College Transition

A Critical Thinking Approach

Susan R. Schapiro, Ph.D.
University at Buffalo, State University of New York

Deborah A. Marinelli
Hudson Valley Community College

EDITED BY Sue Vander Hook

Houghton Mifflin Company
Boston • New York

Director of Student Success Programs and College Survival: Barbara A. Heinssen
Assistant Editor: Shani B. Fisher
Project Editor: Sue Vander Hook
Project Designer: Susan Havice
Manufacturing Manager: Florence Cadran

ACKNOWLEDGMENTS

The authors wish to thank the following people for their contributions to the College Transition project.

The State University of New York for supporting development of the original College Transition Course: John O'Connor (Vice Chancellor of University Life and University Secretary) and the SUNY Board of Trustees; Rick Steiner, Sara Wiest, and Mary Slusarz of the Research Foundation of SUNY; and William J. Murabito of the SUNY Office of University Life

Dr. Schapiro's teaching assistants for excellent insights all along the way: Kelly Ahuna, Christine Tinnesz, Christopher Keegan, Jennifer Livingston, and Kathleen Nieves

Shani Fisher, Barbara A. Heinssen, Tina Miller, Sue Vander Hook, and Alison Zetterquist for supporting the publication of this book

ILLUSTRATION CREDITS

Cover illustration: Thomas Payne; Text illustrations: Debbie Tilley

TEXT CREDITS

Chapter 3: Text in this chapter is adapted from material developed by Ellen J. Langer, author of *Mindfulness* (1989) and *The Power of Mindful Learning* (1997) and is used with her permission.

Chapters 5 and 6: Text in these chapters is adapted from material developed by Claire Ellen Weinstein, Professor of Psychology, University of Texas at Austin, and is used with her permission.

Credits continue on page 290, which constitutes an extension of the copyright page.

Printed in the U. S. A.

ISBN: 0-618-03983-X

1 2 3 4 5 6 7 8 9 0-DOC-04 03 02 01 00

Contents

PART 1

YOUR MIND-
The Foundation For Success

PART 2

COMPREHENSION MONITORING—
Knowing What You Know

Using College Transition

College Transition provides foundation knowledge and strategies for success in higher education and in all life endeavors. It develops the critical thinking and sophisticated learning processes required of today's students and tomorrow's professionals.

College Transition is a personal worktext that guides you to

- analyze your own strengths as a student
- understand what is involved in higher order thinking and learning, and
- become more strategic as you approach all learning tasks—both in and out of school.

Several features of *College Transition* support your learning.

- Activities marked by a **pen-and-paper logo** invite you to actively respond in writing.
- The **Summary** at the end of each chapter highlights key chapter concepts.
- **Let's Talk** chapter-end questions check your understanding of those key concepts, and
- **Apply the Concepts** questions encourage you to go beyond simple understanding and use chapter ideas in new situations.

Although many ideas in this book may be familiar to you, there are new things to learn in every chapter. Even more important, *College Transition* will stimulate your critical thinking and increase your awareness of what it takes to become a successful lifelong learner.

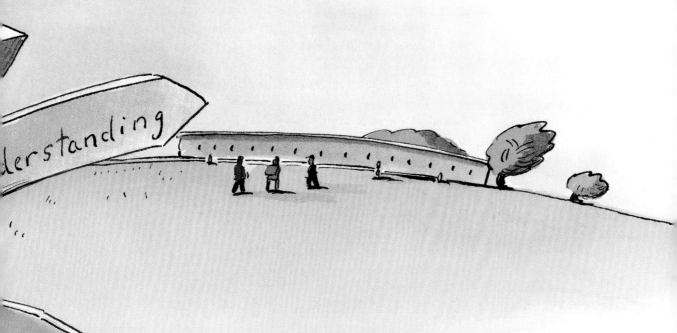

derstanding

ing

Introduction

For centuries people have been trying to unravel the mystery of success. According to Sophocles, "Success is dependent on effort," but Darcy E. Gibbons has declared, "Success is just a matter of attitude." News anchor David Brinkley once said, "A successful person is one who can lay a firm foundation with the bricks that others throw at him or her." We all search for the keys to success every day as we think about how to do things well. You may have already asked yourself: *What can I do to look good today? What will it take to get along with my friends? How can I get a good grade on the algebra test?*

Since you are taking *College Transition*, you probably are interested in succeeding in college. The independence of college life is an experience you've long awaited, but you may be concerned about the responsibilities that come with it. Since being productive in college is usually more difficult than being productive in high school, advanced learning strategies can be very beneficial. In an independent learning situation where knowledge and problem solving are more complex, you will want to be prepared.

College Transition is designed to provide you with a smooth transition from high school to college and to prepare you for the more rigorous demands of higher education. Most importantly, you will discover a higher level of thinking–a focused, organized thought process known as *critical thinking*. You will also master strategic learning techniques such as task management and note taking.

As you become more mindful of your thought patterns and how to use them to learn more effectively, you will begin to think more critically. Becoming aware of how you think will help you improve your abilities to analyze data, make assumptions, reason, draw conclusions, and make judgments. Critical thinking not only prepares your mind for educational achievement, it shapes the reasoning abilities employers desire. Critical thinking will become a practical tool for goal setting and decision making. It will ultimately reshape your entire future.

Success Does Not Depend on Ability

The ability to apply the strategies of *College Transition* successfully does not depend on your scholastic aptitude. Students with average and even low-average scores on standardized tests can often perform as well as students with very high test scores. Enthusiastic and curious average to low-average students often pay close attention and actively involve themselves in the learning process. They learn basic skills and utilize them in all areas of life. As they train their minds to think critically and creatively, their chances for success increase dramatically.

mindset
a mental attitude or inclination that shapes your thinking and your actions

Research and observation show that the right **mindset** for learning and a willingness to work have as great an impact on your education as any natural gift or high IQ. The motivation you bring to your studies and to your career determines the extent to which you will succeed.

Success Is Not Affected by Circumstances

I am what time, circumstance, history, have made of me, certainly, but I am also much more than that. So are we all.

-James Baldwin

You may already have spent much time and energy searching for ways to succeed, perhaps trying to change your circumstances in order to accomplish your goals. Many people believe wealth and a comfortable environment produce exceptional people, but many highly successful people prove that circumstances are not the determining factors of success.

If favorable circumstances were necessary for success, Nelson Mandela would not have achieved very much. Growing up black in South Africa where apartheid produced racial discrimination and oppression, Mandela had little chance to excel. His open opposition to apartheid eventually resulted in 27 years of imprisonment. In spite of his circumstances, he never stopped thinking of ways to develop a multiracial democracy for South Africa. At the age of 75, Mandela's unrelenting determination was rewarded when he was honored with the Nobel Peace Prize. Less than a year later, for the first time in the history of his country, all races voted in a democratic election, choosing Mandela as president of South Africa. Persistence and a passion for the people of his country—not comfort and fortune—accomplished his noble goal.

Success Does Not Depend on Appearance

Just as circumstances do not have to affect your success, your physical appearance does not determine your accomplishments. Many people are convinced that good looks will take them to the top, but appearance played no part in the accomplishments of one of the most dynamic women in the history of the United States.

As one person said of Eleanor Roosevelt, "She was the ugliest woman I ever saw."[1] Though unattractive by society's standards, she became the portrait of one of the most influential female figures of the 20th century. Most people saw past her face and observed an inward beauty—an attractive character.

In addition to her plain appearance, Roosevelt also experienced difficult circumstances. A somewhat bitter childhood, the death of both her parents by the time she was 12, and her extreme shyness could have prevented her from succeeding. Instead, she became a powerful voice for social causes, conducting press conferences, writing a nationally syndicated daily newspaper column, and recording her own radio program. After the death of her husband, President Franklin Delano Roosevelt, she served as a U.S. delegate to the United Nations, helping draft its Declaration of Human Rights.

It may seem strange but no matter how plain a woman may be if truth and loyalty are stamped upon her face all will be attracted to her and she will do good to all who come near her and those who know her will always love her for they will feel her loyal spirit and have confidence in her while another woman far more beautiful and attractive will never gain anybody's confidence simply because those around her feel lack of loyalty.

-Eleanor Roosevelt
(written at age 14)

[1] Cook, B.W. *Eleanor Roosevelt: Volume 1, 1884–1933.* Penguin USA; 1993.

Success Comes From Within

Although circumstances may condition you, appearance may affect your confidence, and others may influence you, the essential ingredient for success remains *within you*. The way you think helps you accomplish your goals and realize your potential. Learning how to think critically puts you in control of applying what you learn. It gives you power over your education, your future career, and every aspect of your life.

Power can be a threatening idea, especially if you are not the one in power. The word often reminds us of someone taking advantage of another person, or of a nation exerting force over a weaker nation. Power is actually a noble idea when applied to an individual who uses it to shape his or her own life. The power to form your learning into a satisfying, successful experience is found within you, in a place where only you can go–your mind. People who recognize that this **locus** of control is within them can determine the direction of their future and convince others to help them along the way. That is real power.

locus
the place where something is situated or occurs; a center of activity

At a time when you, as a student, must be more powerful–learning faster and producing more–*College Transition* offers valuable insights, thinking strategies, practical instruction, and self-assessment skills to help you realize your own potential. This course will ease you into your college education and prepare you for a successful future. Applying its concepts will liberate you from the trap of being a passive recipient of knowledge and put you in control of your own learning process. As you become actively involved in learning, your chances for success will be unlimited. The locus of control is within you!

College Transition

A Critical Thinking Approach

Part 1

Your Mind—
The Foundation for Success

The Four Basic Properties of the Mind

Helen Keller was an extraordinary woman who used her mind to emerge from a dark, silent world of blindness and deafness to become an author, lecturer, and suffragist. Her life serves as an invitation to realize the potential of your own mind—the place where thinking and ideas begin—and calls you to tap into your own powerful source of learning.

Becoming a powerful learner is what *College Transition* is about. Although educational institutions provide the tools and the resources for learning, within each individual lie the power and the ability to learn. The purpose of this course is not to discover all of the multifaceted aspects of the brain, but rather to show how several basic properties of the mind can work together to ensure successful learning and successful living.

The mind is not a vessel to be filled but a fire to be kindled.
    –Plutarch

The Properties at Work

property
a quality or trait belonging to an individual or a thing

The mind possesses many qualities, but for the purpose of this course, we will discuss four of its basic **properties**: *Drive, Action, Openness,* and *Reason*. We should not be surprised that Helen Keller's success was based on her intense development of these four basic properties of the mind.

A closer study of Helen Keller's life reveals how she started with the first property of the mind—*Drive*. Though often manifested in anger and tantrums, her relentless desire to "know" drove her to seek persistently after knowledge. As you would expect, this natural drive to learn was followed by the second property of the mind—*Action*. She discovered many amazing things she could do with what she had learned. As her learning abilities progressed to higher levels of thinking, she used the third property of her mind—*Openness*. Throughout her later education, she increasingly became aware of her ability to interpret data, compare ideas, consider different interpretations of ideas, and understand things correctly.

Fortunately for the world, Helen Keller's phenomenal use of her mind did not stop with openness. With the first three properties as a foundation, she tapped into the fourth property of the mind—*Reason*. Based on the best information and the best logic, she finally learned to make distinctions and determine significance. She spoke out for justice and better pay for the working class and demanded equal rights for women. She helped set up the American Foundation for the Blind in order to provide better services for people with impaired vision.

> When we do the best that we can, we never know what miracle is wrought in our life, or in the life of another.
> -Helen Keller

Your Own Mind

Your values and your decisions will probably be different from those of Helen Keller. Yet within you is the power to make use of the same basic properties of your mind in order to accomplish your goals and direct your future.

The next four chapters cover each of the four basic properties of the mind in more detail. As you study them, do not focus on how you have perceived your own level of intelligence in the past. Nor should you think about how others have previously tested your level of knowledge or characterized your intellect. Focus instead on the limitless possibilities available to you by utilizing and taking control of this amazing power source—your mind.

Four Basic Properties of the Mind

 Drive

"I want to know."

~ Natural Enthusiasm
~ Curiosity
~ Adventure
~ Persistence

 Action

"I'm ready to get to work."

~ Gathers Data
~ Asks Questions
~ Makes Sense of Problems
~ Uses Feedback

 Openness

"Am I understanding well?"

~ Compares
~ Interprets
~ Searches for Meaning
~ Stays Open to New Ideas

 Reason

"I can think logically."

~ Sees the "Big Picture"
~ Determines Significance
~ Identifies Options
~ Chooses Wisely

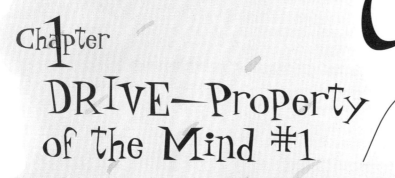

Chapter **1**

DRIVE—Property of the Mind #1

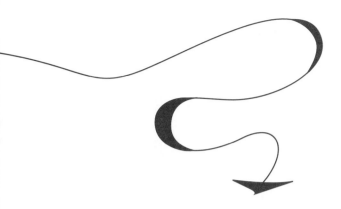

As a young child, you were naturally very curious. You probably picked up everything in sight—examining, testing, and even tasting each item. Objects got squeezed, tossed, and rolled. You gave them strange names and let your imagination run free. Learning was fun; it was a game that lasted from the time you got up until you fell into bed exhausted.

*Most would certainly agree that children like to learn. Children are natural, fearless learners, always eager to find out new things. Children use this **innate** desire to learn randomly, enjoying each new discovery. Everything they do is driven by a **disposition** to investigate energetically and enthusiastically.*

Your Natural Learning Drive

Two recent studies demonstrate that natural learning drive leads to academic success. The authors of these studies call it "**dynamic** self-regulation."[1] Simply stated, it is an energetic way of wanting to learn. Consider your own inborn desire to learn. Think back about what you enjoyed doing as a child. What activities sparked your curiosity and created enthusiasm? Under what circumstances were you willing to take risks? What activity allowed you to adventure into new mental territory? What was your style for completing a task—getting it done in record speed or finishing it slowly and persistently? Whatever your interests and your learning styles were, you undoubtedly depended a lot on the first basic property of your mind—drive. You abounded in enthusiasm, curiosity, adventure, and persistence.

innate
inborn; existing in an individual from birth

disposition
a mental outlook or mood; an inclination or tendency

dynamic
energetic and forceful; characterized by continuous and productive activity

[1] Iran-Nejad, A. and B. S. Chissom, "Contributions of Active and Dynamic Self-Regulation to Learning." *Innovative Higher Education*, 17, 1992; pp. 125–136.

Schapiro, S. and J. Livingston "Dynamic Self-Regulation: The Driving Force Behind Academic Achievement." 1999. Under review.

Your Natural Learning Drive

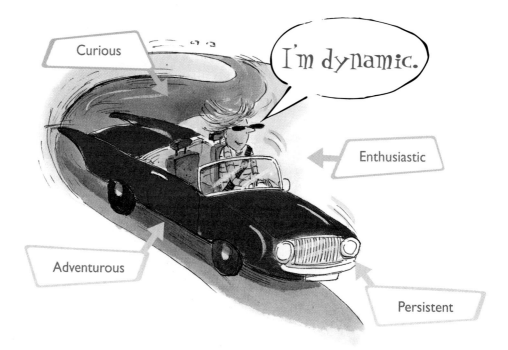

Curious

I'm dynamic.

Enthusiastic

Adventurous

Persistent

What Happened to Your Desire for Learning?

Many situations can discourage instinctive, spontaneous discovery. Often without realizing it, a person may fall into the drudgery of learning facts without understanding their applications. The list below describes some of the things that may have dulled your natural learning drive. Which ones apply to you?

- ~ I was told "No" too many times.
- ~ Someone made me stop investigating things (too dangerous).
- ~ I couldn't find anything to take apart.
- ~ I was told to stop asking so many questions.
- ~ I wasn't allowed to talk during adult conversations.
- ~ I just became more careful.
- ~ I stopped taking risks.
- ~ I decided it's not cool to be smart.
- ~ My friends thought learning was stupid.

- Someone made fun of my enthusiasm for learning.
- I was forced into **rote** learning.
- Too much "busy work" in school left no time for investigative learning.
- My grades became more important than learning.

rote
mere repetition of memorized words or facts without thought for meaning

In "growing up," you may have become a well-behaved child and a delight to adults and friends around you, but how much childlike enthusiasm did you lose along the way? As you got older and more sophisticated, how much of your quest for knowledge was replaced by a quest for approval?

Now that you are about to face the rigors of higher education, you will most likely need to rediscover your natural learning drive. Taking control of your learning begins with reclaiming your desire to chase after knowledge. Following are some specific ways to tap into your learning power.

Reclaiming Your Natural Learning Drive

BE ENTHUSIASTIC It's always easier to be enthusiastic about something if you are passionate about it. When you *choose* to do a task, its value increases significantly in your mind and your chance for success multiplies greatly. At the beginning of the school year, there is usually one class you look forward to. More than likely, you will get your highest grade in that class because you approach the course *enthusiastically*.

If you want to accomplish the goals of your life, you have to begin with the spirit.

-Oprah Winfrey

USEFUL TIPS:

- Challenge yourself to be enthusiastic about your classes. *(Example: Make the decision to find something interesting or completely new about each class.)*
- Actively turn study drudgery into fun (be creative). *(Example: Use your vocabulary words in everyday speech.) (Example: Write a song or a poem using vocabulary words.)*
- Get rid of negative attitudes. *(Example: For two weeks, say only positive things about your classes. When a negative thought occurs, replace it with a positive thought. Think up a creative solution if a problem arises in one of your classes.)*

BE CURIOUS Another way to reclaim your natural learning power is to investigate every new thing curiously. As a child, you explored thoroughly, mastering new facts, words, and ideas with delight. You spotted people along the way, easily making friends with them. Curiosity can give a subject a new dimension and transform worn-out ideas into brand new opinions.

USEFUL TIPS:

- ~ Take a long look at yourself in the mirror. Discover something you've never noticed.
- ~ Take a long look at one of your friends and find something you've never noticed before.
- ~ Choose your least favorite subject. Use the Internet to discover a totally new fact about it. Share it with someone.
- ~ Tip your head sideways and look at a friend. What do you see that's different than before?
- ~ Carefully observe an insect. Compare it to something. *(Example: Does the insect look like a person—like anyone you know?)*

BE ADVENTUROUS Yet another aspect of your natural learning drive is your willingness to take risks. Being ready to go mentally where you've never gone before will transform learning into an adventure. Some people are natural risk-takers, bungee jumping from high bridges and free falling from airplanes. Although they may seem foolish, they do experience an incredible thrill for testing their limits. Have the courage to take a learning risk, testing the limits of your own mind.

USEFUL TIPS:

- ~ Think about the craziest dream you've ever had. Write five great sentences about it, and then let someone read them.
- ~ While doing your homework, listen to a different style of music for each subject.
- ~ For your next report, use the Internet, mail, or telephone to contact the author of one of the books you're using for research. Be ready to ask the author some questions about the subject you're writing about. Give an account of your "meeting" in class or in your report.
- ~ Ask a question in your hardest class.
- ~ At your next party or get-together, ask someone a challenging intellectual question. Keep the conversation going as long as you can.

BE PERSISTENT Remember the slow tortoise that beat the fast hare in the race? What was the tortoise's secret? It was **persistence**. Research shows that those who "plug along" often achieve considerable success (and even outperform the "sprinters"). If you hurry through a task, you may miss many opportunities and waste your time learning only surface information.

Taking time to pursue a goal thoroughly will increase your chances of finishing with satisfaction. Slow and steady perseverance can triumph over a short-term power surge. Even if you encounter frustrating problems, stay with your course long enough to give yourself time to reach your goal. You will enjoy the final result—success.

persistence
the quality of continuing steadfastly or stubbornly in spite of opposition

Slow and steady wins the race.
    -Aesop

USEFUL TIPS:

~ Buy (for real or not) some stock in your favorite company. Don't "sell" it for at least a year.
~ Start a learning journal. Promise to write in it every day for six months. Write down some of the ways you are reclaiming your natural drive to learn.
~ For one week, do all your homework where you cannot see a clock. Enjoy having ample time to learn.

Summary

Because the drive to learn is a natural trait, it does not just fade away. Enthusiasm, curiosity, adventure, and persistence are innate inclinations that naturally result in energetic, enthusiastic learning. Your natural learning drive may be suppressed, either by outside influences or by your own choices, but it can be reclaimed and put back into action.

There are four basic ways to tap into your natural learning drive. The first is to learn enthusiastically—make the choice to turn boredom into excitement and drudgery into enjoyment. The second is to be curious about new things—to explore them thoroughly, mastering new facts and ideas. Curiosity sheds new light on worn-out concepts and enriches your perception.

The third way to regain your natural learning drive is to make learning an adventure—take academic risks and explore new mental territory. The fourth way is to be persistent—do not always depend on short-term power surges, but give yourself time to pursue an assignment or a goal thoroughly and enjoy the success that will follow. These four basic ways of returning to the enjoyment of child-like discovery will set in motion the kind of higher-level learning that you will need in college and in your future career.

1. How would you explain "innate learning drive"? Why might this kind of learning lead to success?

2. Take five minutes to examine your own drive to learn. Share at least one way in which you are already using your natural learning drive.

3. Explain how learning would be different for you if *enthusiasm* were left out completely. What if *curiosity* were the missing trait? What would learning be like without *adventure*? How would things change if *persistence* were absent? If you had to get rid of one of these four characteristics of natural learning drive, which one do you think you could do without?

Apply the Concepts

1. Look back at the list on pages 6 and 7. Divide a sheet of paper into two columns. Label one column "Things That Have Dulled My Natural Learning Drive." Label the other column "What I Can Do to Reclaim My Natural Learning Drive." In the first column, determine why you lost your drive to learn (you may have reasons in addition to those on the list). In the second column, describe specific things you can do to take back your natural learning drive.

2. On the basis of the lists you developed in question 1 above, honestly evaluate your own strengths and weaknesses as a learner.

3. In your opinion, how important is a natural drive to learn? (*Circle the spot on the continuum below to show how important it is to you.*) Explain your response.

Completely unnecessary	Useful at times	Relevant only in school	Absolutely essential	The key to success

__|_____|____|____|____|____|____|____|____|____|_

4. Julia Child advised, "Find something you're passionate about and keep tremendously interested in it." What is one thing you could say you are passionate about? How do you plan to "keep tremendously interested" in it?

Chapter 2
ACTION—Property of the Mind #2

Action Gets Things Done

Four Learning Strategies

Applying the Strategies

Summary

Your natural learning drive, though essential, does not stand alone in the learning process. Drive by itself is full of energy, but it is not focused. Its momentum however, can carry you to the next important property of the mind—Action.

Action Gets Things Done

The drive to learn is like a beautiful wild horse thrashing and bucking in a corral. Its powerful energy is put to better use when someone trains it and disciplines it to use its strength intentionally. Natural talent can also thrash about uselessly if it has no direction. That is why gifted musicians practice tirelessly for a competition and athletes train intensely for an event. Ballerinas stretch until it hurts, and artists paint long after inspiration subsides.

You, too, can get things done by harnessing your natural learning energy to make it perform to your advantage. *Drive* is an exciting adventure in learning, but *Action* is the practical effort that links knowledge to everyday life. Since *Action* emphasizes effectiveness, you can, with great confidence, make workable plans and strategize to carry them out. Once you harness your natural enthusiasm and put it to work, you can discover what learning strategies will help you excel.

Carpe diem!
(Seize the day!)

-Horace

Four Learning Strategies

There are four basic learning strategies that will improve your performance and enhance achievement as you reach for educational goals. These basic strategies also can be applied to occupational, social, and personal goals. As you look at the following learning strategies, relate the strategies to a particularly difficult class you may be taking right now. You can also apply these strategies to classes you plan to take in college.

Four Learning Strategies

Make Sense of the Data

Often the purpose of a course gets lost in the clutter of information. Making sense of the data in order to understand the usefulness of the subject often seems difficult, if not impossible. Believing a course is worthwhile depends on realizing the importance of its content.

Strategy: Discover the questions the course is asking.

Example: If you want to understand the value of psychology or sociology, look at the questions those subjects ask. Psychology asks about the mind and behavior of individuals. Sociology asks about the functioning of groups or society.

Strategy: Discover the method that experts in the subject use to answer its questions.

Example: Experts in physics usually diagram their problems before they state their theories. On the other hand, anthropologists search for sites and dig to find physical data to develop their theories.

Find Out What's Going On

Every subject is made up of information (data) and its interpretation. In order to find out what a course is really about, look at the information in light of other surrounding circumstances and keep the data in the right context.

Strategy: Look at the parts (bits of data), then put them together to see the whole, OR Look at the whole, and then see how the parts fit into it.

Example: Most subjects require you to keep in mind the parts and the whole. Architecture is a good example. Architects work with blueprints made up of squares, circles, and other representative shapes without much meaning on their own. But take a look at the building that results from those drawings and you will understand and appreciate the function of those once meaningless shapes on the paper. The well-constructed building would not have been possible without all the pieces of the plan.

Get Into Your Instructor's Head

No matter what course you take, the subject will contain too much information for a teacher to cover in a single semester. As a result, your instructor will have to choose what he or she thinks are the most important things to emphasize. Another instructor may choose different information to cover. The materials your teacher chooses reflect the course objectives.

Strategy: Use the course objectives to determine what will be on tests.

Example: Although you don't want to learn only what will be on a test (you might miss a lot of good information), it makes sense to prepare for tests by getting into your instructor's head—knowing what he or she considers important.

Strategy: Be certain you understand your instructor. It is not necessary to agree with her or him.

Example: You may strongly disagree with some things your instructors say. That's fine—you are not obligated to believe everything you are taught. Try to understand where your instructors are coming from by listening to the reasons they teach or think in a particular way, however.

Utilize Feedback

Talking gives learning a boost. Inviting feedback from teachers and other students will enhance your learning opportunities. Many students think of learning as a solitary activity, but working with another person or a team can offer advantages. A study partner may see things you have missed, or perhaps you will notice something your partner has missed. Several people working as a team can usually sort through information and material more effectively.

Strategy: Study regularly with a partner or a team.

Example: Ask each other questions, share notes, make up test questions.

Strategy: If you can't meet with a partner or group, try "self-talk."

Example: Make comments to yourself and prompt yourself to react to material. ("I'm not sure I buy into that idea" or "Just what I always suspected!") This gives you the feeling of team power.

Do some self-testing by asking yourself questions that you believe your teacher will ask.

Applying the Strategies

In order for the four learning strategies to be effective, you need to apply them to your own specific circumstances. For example, you may struggle with a course like English literature because you do not understand how it could apply to your area of interest, which might be computer science. In addition, you may have trouble keeping up with course assignments or getting good grades on tests. You do know, however, that English literature is a required course for graduation. In these circumstances, how might you strategize for success?

The first step is to tap into the first property of the mind—*Drive*. Choosing to be enthusiastic, curious, adventurous, and persistent in a difficult course will give you the necessary momentum to apply the second property of the mind—*Action*. Now you are ready to focus, strategize, and discipline yourself to get the job done by applying the Four Learning Strategies to your problematic class.

Use the following chart to plan and strategize for one of your difficult educational situations. If you do not have a class with some special challenges at the present time, then choose a course in which your interest is rather low.

Applying Four Learning Strategies

My plan for applying the Four Learning Strategies

Difficult class: _____

1 **Make Sense of the Data**	2 **Find Out What's Going On**	3 **Get Into Your Instructor's Head**	4 **Utilize Feedback**
What questions is the course asking? _____ _____ _____	What are the "parts" (bits of information) in this course? _____ _____ _____	What does my instructor consider the most important things about this course (the course objectives)? _____ _____ _____	What other student in the class might be a good study partner for me? _____ _____ _____
What methods do the experts use to answer the questions of the course? _____ _____ _____ _____			What are the names of several students I could study with as a team? _____ _____ _____
	When I fit the parts together, what "big picture" do I see? _____ _____ _____	Now that I understand what my instructor thinks is important, what information do I think might be on the next test? _____ _____ _____	
Perhaps what I learn from this course will not be used directly in my chosen field. How might this course enrich other areas of my life? _____ _____ _____			When I prefer not to study with someone else, what feedback can I obtain through "self-talk" questions? What questions can I ask myself that the teacher will probably ask? _____ _____ _____

Summary

Putting your natural learning drive into action may be the most important thing you need to do as you prepare for higher-level learning. Once you understand that you are in charge of the direction your learning will take, you can then focus on the strategies that will get the job done. Using the second property of your mind—*Action*—will allow you to accomplish what you set out to do. Whether making a social plan for the next hour or a career choice for the rest of your life, your strategy is the same—harness the energy of your natural learning drive and discipline it to do the work.

Since your major priority right now is probably to improve school performance, these learning strategies provide a good place to start (see pages 15–16):

1. **MAKE SENSE OF THE DATA** Understanding the usefulness of a subject depends upon making sense of the information. Judging a course on the basis of a clutter of data will obscure the real importance of its content.

2. **FIND OUT WHAT'S GOING ON** Finding out what a course is really about is determined by how you interpret the data. It is important to look at information in the right context and in light of other surrounding circumstances.

3. **GET INTO YOUR INSTRUCTOR'S HEAD** An instructor chooses what he or she thinks is the most important information to emphasize in a course. These materials determine the course objectives. Understanding what your instructor has chosen as the course content will help you focus your studies on the information likely to be tested. You may also want to talk to your instructor about what you can do to prepare for a test.

4. **UTILIZE FEEDBACK** Feedback from others helps you sort through information and material more efficiently. It gives you the opportunity to realize things you have missed or point out something another person has overlooked. When you prefer not to study with other students, "self-talk," or prompting yourself to react to the material, will provide effective feedback.

Let's Talk

1. How would you describe the property of your mind called *Action*? Which of the characteristics of that property are you already using? Which ones do you need to work on?

2. What does it mean to "develop a strategy"? What is the function or purpose of a strategy?

3. What does it mean to "get into your instructor's head"? Discuss the benefits of using this strategy.

4. What are the major advantages of studying with a partner or a team? What are the major advantages of studying alone?

5. What kind of "self-talk" questions might help you better prepare for tests?

Apply the Concepts

1. Write a brief explanation of what learning would be like if you left strategy out of your learning process.

2. Think of one class that is especially challenging right now. Write a description of several ways you can actively get the job done in that class. (Come up with some new strategies you will use in addition to the four learning strategies in this chapter.)

3. Learning strategies can also be applied to the development of your natural talents. Write a paragraph explaining one of your natural talents. Then write about your strategy for developing it and using it in the course of your life.

4. How might the four learning strategies in this chapter apply to a job or career? Be specific.

5. Using the learning strategies on pages 15 and 16 as a basis, create four "social strategies" for solving difficult interpersonal relationships (i.e. parent/child, boy/girl, friends, peers, etc.).

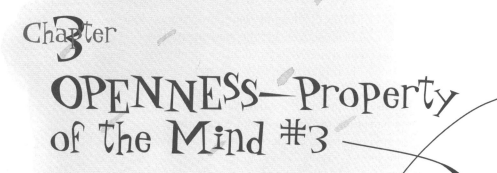

Chapter 3

OPENNESS—Property of the Mind #3

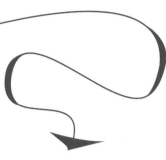

In the first two chapters of this course, you discovered how to put your natural learning drive to work for you. Energy and hard work may already be helping you enjoy your learning experience. By now, you may be employing practical learning strategies and improving classroom performance. At this point, you're ready for some higher-level thinking with a more complex property of your mind—Openness.

Learning With Openness

Perhaps the best way to define learning with openness is to define first what it is not—it is not single-minded thinking or seeing only one aspect of an idea at a time. Single-minded thinking does involve brain activity, but only on one level. It may be able to answer the *who*, the *what*, the *where*, the *when*, and the *why* (when the answer is clear), but it does not view the answers with any **perspective**. Single-minded thinking does not produce reasonable conclusions that reflect depth of understanding. Thinking on one level may help you win a trivia contest, but it will not take you to higher levels of thought or substance in the same way that open thinking will.

Open thinking releases you from the monotony of **rote learning** and frees you to consider many different viewpoints and perspectives. At this higher level of thinking, you are able to give meaning to apparently random information by recognizing the differences and similarities among ideas.

Minds are like parachutes. They only function when open.

-Lord Thomas Dewar

perspective
the capacity to view things according to their importance or as they relate to each other

rote learning
learning that is done by routine or repetitious memorization, usually with little application

pattern
a distinct logical system based on the interrelationship of component parts

Oh, would that my mind could let fall its dead ideas, as the tree does its withered leaves!

-Learned Hand

Giving order to facts begins with a meaningful search for **patterns**. When you perceive patterns, you can organize bits of information and understand how they relate to each other. Once you comprehend the association of apparently jumbled facts, you will soon discover their meaning and significance.

As new information comes to light, meanings and ideas may change. Facts that once fit together nicely may demand reorganization. A search for a new pattern will begin, and new ideas will be formulated. Digging deeper and learning more are important aspects of openness. An open thinker will eagerly compare old patterns with new information in order to develop a valid basis for new assumptions and changed points of view.

Using the following chart, compare single-minded thinking with open thinking. Consider how you can become more open in your thought processes. Keep in mind that open thinking applies not only to educational issues, but also to occupational, social, and personal issues.

Single-Minded Thinking

- looks at the world from a single perspective.

- recalls information; stops at surface understanding.

- reaches a conclusion after considering only one viewpoint.

- believes facts without determining their validity.

- judges the present by oversimplifying the past.

- pays no attention to context.

- makes hasty decisions based on feelings alone.

- reluctant to modify a decision.

- _____

Open Thinking

- sees the world as many parts that make up a whole.

- uses information to formulate new ideas; digs deeper, asks questions.

- reaches a conclusion after weighing the soundness of many different viewpoints.

- draws distinctions and makes comparisons

- learns from the past to make better decisions in the present.

- looks at the surrounding circumstances before judging a person or a situation.

- understands the facts and options clearly before making a decision.

- willingly compares past choices with new information to consider new decisions.

- _____

You can break down open thinking into four basic processes.

Open thinking involves...

- ❖ **searching for patterns**
- ❖ **exploring hypothetical thinking**
- ❖ **acknowledging uncertainty**
- ❖ **recognizing the need for change**

Searching for Patterns

Perhaps the most fundamental characteristic of an open thinker is his or her willingness to search actively for patterns. Openness involves the challenge of solving a sort of puzzle formed by a collection of data. Searching for patterns is much like the childhood experience of connecting the dots. To a young child, a dot-to-dot challenge may appear unsolvable—a confusing array. But as a child puts order to the dots and connects them in a prearranged pattern, suddenly the dots take on shape and meaning. They lose their randomness and reveal the once obscured picture. The picture was always there, but you had to know how to properly connect the dots in order to see it.

So it is with the figurative "dots" that make up the vast array of facts, information, statistics, numbers, and miscellaneous data in your mind. The "picture" is always there. But the facts must be properly connected to have significance.

> A man may have a great mass of knowledge, but if he has not worked it up by thinking it over for himself, it has much less value than a far smaller amount which he has thoroughly pondered.
>
> -Arthur Schopenhauer

Below is a random distribution of words from a biology class. At first glance, they have no order or meaning. But in the table below notice how the words take on significance when they are grouped into categories.

genes radiation therapy bone marrow transplant
mustard gas
mutation PCBs ribosomes
lymph stem cells
lindane DNA cell chemotherapy
blood transfusion autologous transplant Golgi bodies radiation seeding
radiation follicles oncology
benzene dioxin stem cell transplants
DDT membrane interferon

Human Cell	Carcinogens That Affect the Human Cell	Cancer Treatments
cell	PCBs	oncology
membrane	lindane	blood transfusion
genes	dioxin	chemotherapy
DNA	benzene	autologous transplant
lymph	radiation	radiation therapy
follicles	mustard gas	radiation seeding
stem cells	DDT	bone marrow transplant
ribosomes		interferon
Golgi bodies		stem cell transplants
mutation		

Once these words were just a hodgepodge of terms. Now they have shape and meaning. The figurative "dots" have formed a "picture"—a pattern. With the pattern now in place, you can compare and contrast facts, discover how they work together, and agree or disagree with the ideas they convey. If, for instance, you had already carefully learned the definitions of these words, the patterns formed by the chart would be especially meaningful and useful. With your prior knowledge and your organized pattern, you could easily write a sound essay on cancer.

The construction of patterns is essential as you organize written assignments in subjects like English and history. It is also critical to designing and implementing advanced experimentation in the sciences. As your thinking becomes more open, you will most likely see your high school work improve. In college, open thinking will greatly increase the quality of your coursework.

Exploring Hypothetical Thinking

Discovering a pattern allows you to better understand your store of information. You may even make some assumptions and establish your own viewpoints from your pattern. But what if another person with the same information were to come up with an opposing viewpoint? What if someone challenged your assumptions? Would you be able to defend your findings? You may need more information and more open thinking to support your statements. More than likely, you will need to explore hypothetical thinking. Simply put, **hypothetical** thinking is asking yourself, *"What if . . .?"*

hypothetical
referring to a tentative assumption made in order to draw out and test its logical consequences

In an educational setting, a teacher usually asks for your ideas and assumptions based on the information you have. However, a teacher may also ask you to put the information into a hypothetical situation. For example, suppose you were studying the novel *The Scarlet Letter* in an English literature class. Presume you have read the book, identified the characters, and thoroughly studied the plot and its implications. You may have considered solutions to the moral dilemma of the main characters in light of their Puritan backgrounds. A teacher may push your thought processes even further by asking a question like this:

"What if Hester Prynne and Arthur Dimmesdale were not Puritans? How might the story be different?"

In response to the question, you would first need more information about Puritans and the society and time in which they lived. You would need to imagine what other options the characters in this novel would have had if, in fact, they were not bound to Puritan values. Responses to this hypothetical situation would probably vary throughout the class. One student might be convinced that without their Puritan restrictions, Hester and Arthur surely would run away together and live happily ever after. Someone else may believe they would make the same decisions based upon their own **intrinsic** senses of right and wrong. Another student may have yet another point of view.

As you explore hypothetical thinking, you may not necessarily arrive at conclusions. *"What if . . .?"* questions broaden your understanding and vary your points of view. Exploring this level of thinking will require you to take some risks. Along the way, you will also need to acknowledge some uncertainty.

> The wise, though all laws were abolished, would lead the same life.
>
> -Aristophanes

intrinsic
belonging to someone by their basic, essential nature

Acknowledging Uncertainty

- -

Acknowledging uncertainty is recognizing that final answers are rare. New information will change many of your conclusions. New discoveries will alter patterns and modify solutions. Think back on the pattern formed from the array of words on cancer (see page 27). Scientists are continually finding new causes for cancer, as well as new and better cancer treatments. As cancer information changes, you will need to realize that your hypotheses and assumptions about cancer cannot remain fixed.

Since you will rarely have all the information on a given subject or issue, uncertainty is very likely. The following four steps may be helpful as you deal with uncertainty.

> There is no good reason why we should not develop and change until the last day we live.
>
> -Karen Horney

- ~ Gather the best information available.
- ~ Process your information with open thinking.
- ~ Hypothesize a temporary assumption based on the best information.
- ~ Be willing to look at new information, search for new patterns, and recognize the need for change.

Recognizing the Need for Change

Changing a carefully formulated idea should not be viewed as a failure. Change does not necessarily mean that your first assumptions were wrong. Recognizing the need for change is simply acknowledging that new information can lead to new conclusions.

For example, your decision to go to a particular college will be based upon careful investigation. After reading catalogs, looking at course lists and faculty, and perhaps visiting campuses, you will make what you assume to be a good college choice. However, after attending that college for a year, you may feel it is really not right for you. The student population may not seem friendly, or the courses and teachers may fall short of your expectations.

That is not the time to consider yourself unsuccessful and quit school. It is time to acknowledge your uncertainty and examine the new information you gained over the past year. The following steps will be helpful in determining the need for change:

1. Acknowledge uncertainty
2. Gather new information
3. Reorganize the facts
4. Search for new patterns
5. Explore hypothetical situations
6. Make a new decision

Determining the Need for Change

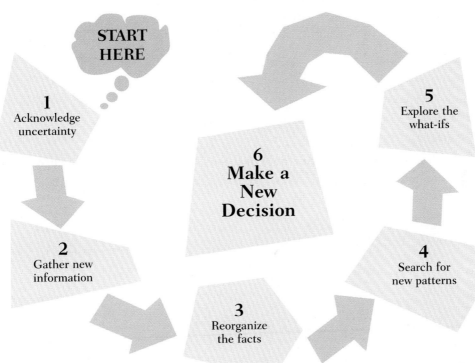

The following chart is an example of how you can put the above steps into practice. The example of dissatisfaction with grades at school is used in the chart, but you can easily use this method for any decision-making process. Keep in mind that your final decision may be the same as your previous one. For example, after closely examining your present college situation in light of new insights on other colleges, you may decide that staying there is still your best choice.

Example

Managing Change

Concern: dissatisfaction with grades at school

Acknowledge uncertainty.
not sure of the reasons why grades aren't better

Gather new information.
Check out *College Transition* table of contents. Are there elements of academic success I'm missing? Ask instructors.

Reorganize the facts and search for new patterns. (Perhaps change priorities.)
It seems like I'm not spending enough study time to succeed.

Facts: Here's how I spend my day now.		Reorganization: Here are my priorities.	
Sports	4 hours	School	6 hours
School activities	2 hours	Chores for family	1 hour
Chores for family	1 hour	Travel	1 hour
School	6 hours	Sleeping	8 hours
Travel	1 hour	Eating	2 hours = 18 hours
Sleeping	8 hours	Studying	?
Eating	2 hours = 24 hours	Sports	?
Studying	no time left	School activities	?

Explore the what-ifs.
I have six hours left in my day after the must-dos. How much time can I reserve for studying? What if I cut out all school activities except sports? What if I cut back on sports? What if I eat while driving or study during lunch?

Make a new decision.
Find time to put in at least 3 hours a day studying. It doesn't have to be all at once. Drop one sport. Take part in some school activities that combine with lunch. Find time in the school day (between classes? before class?) to do some studying.

Now work on a problem you are having.

Managing Change

Concern: _____

Acknowledge uncertainty.

_____

Gather new information.

_____

_____

Reorganize the facts and search for new patterns. (Perhaps change priorities.)

_____

_____

_____

_____

_____

_____

_____

_____

_____

_____

_____

_____

_____

Explore the what-ifs.

_____

_____

Make a new decision.

_____

_____

_____

_____

_____

Summary

Open thinking—thinking past bare facts—is vital to educational, occupational, social, and personal success. Teachers, coaches, employers, parents, and friends all encourage you to use rational understanding. Great personal satisfaction can be gained by moving from fact to comprehension. In all probability, your grades will improve, and you will reach higher levels of achievement in other activities as well. Maintaining your openness will no doubt diminish boredom as you look at things with new awareness and receptiveness. Knowing what to do with information to make it interesting and meaningful will keep you motivated to learn.

The process of learning with openness begins by moving from single-minded thinking to open thinking. Open thinking releases you to consider diverse points of view and various perspectives in your search for truth. It allows you to move beyond a mere recollection of facts to a more detailed and complex thought process. Instead of accepting facts in an unchanging context, an open thinker will compare them to other facts, note the differences and similarities, and determine their relationships. The result is powerful, more complete understanding.

There are four basic processes that facilitate learning with openness:

1. Search for patterns
2. Explore hypothetical thinking
3. Acknowledge uncertainty
4. Recognize the need for change

When you arrange an array of information into patterns, facts take on meaning and significance. Understanding follows naturally. Exploring hypothetical thinking, a higher level of open thinking, will test your understanding. At the same time, you will broaden your comprehension and vary your points of view.

An essential part of exploring hypothetical thinking is acknowledging uncertainty, or recognizing that final answers are rare. Because discoveries cast new light on old facts, you will need to alter your assumptions and choices from time to time. New information will cause you to reprocess data repeatedly, reformulate patterns, and recognize that change may be necessary. An open thinker allows new discoveries to change assumptions.

It is important to remember that amended conclusions and decisions are not an indication of failure. On the contrary, your willingness to alter your course of action, based upon relevant information, will increase your chances for academic, occupational, and social success.

Let's Talk

1. Discuss some of the differences between single-minded thinking and open thinking.

2. How is searching for patterns like solving a puzzle? Explain how a completed pattern might be compared to a picture.

3. What type of question does a hypothetical situation ask? Give three examples of a hypothetical question.

4. How do you know when you should change your mind? Change your conclusion? Explain the process of modifying a decision.

Apply the Concepts

1. Discuss how openness affects the way you think. List at least five examples.

2. Make two columns on a piece of paper. Label the left column "Single-Minded Thinking" and the right column "Open Thinking." For a period of one week, keep a log of the way you think. When you find yourself thinking single mindedly, note the situation and how you are seeing only one aspect of a thought or an idea. Likewise, note when you are thinking openly, considering different viewpoints and perspectives. At the end of the week, turn in your log along with several written paragraphs that explain how you tend to think. Describe ways you can develop more open thinking.

3. Your teacher may ask you to explore hypothetical situations on an assignment or test. You can also ask yourself hypothetical questions (*what ifs*) as you study. Choose one of your academic classes and write five hypothetical questions that would enhance your comprehension in the subject.

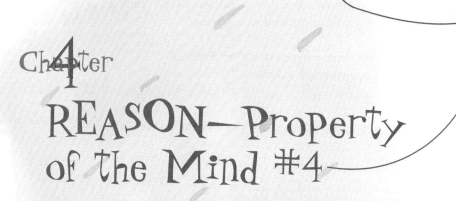

Chapter 4

REASON—Property of the Mind #4

Thinking with Reason

Reasoning and Critical Thinking

Filtering Choices

Using a Critical-Thinking Plan

Summary

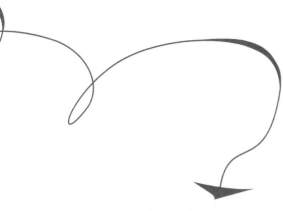

Chapters 1 through 3 have taken you on a journey from natural learning drive to strategic action and on to understanding. The road to comprehension may have seemed like the end of your intellectual journey or the final destination on your way to real knowledge. Understanding, however, is not the final property of thinking.

Thinking With Reason

Your mind is capable of incorporating yet another property—*Reason*. To reason is to think things through in a logical manner in order to form **inferences** or conclusions. Reasoning is the ability to think **critically**. Many people relate the word *critical* to the act of criticizing or finding fault. But when used to describe a thought process, *critical* refers to your ability to make careful judgments and sensible evaluations. As you think critically, you determine your own core values and form opinions.

Perhaps you have already begun to enjoy freedom from dry facts and rote learning. You may have discovered that taking the extra time to explore concepts and hypothetical questions produces benefits that far outweigh the effort. With open thinking, you learned to form patterns from an array of information in order to compare and contrast facts and to make assumptions. Now, as you begin to think more critically, you will be able to look at the big picture in order to evaluate it.

There is an old saying that claims, "You can't see the forest for the trees."

inference
something concluded by reasoning from known facts or evidence

critically
in a manner relating to careful judgment or sensible evaluation

It is not best that we all should think alike, it is differences of opinion that make horse races.

-Mark Twain

Knowledge is true opinion.

-Plato

It means that you are not able to step back from the details and see the big picture. The individual trees are beautiful, but the forest is spectacular. If you can see the big picture and form an opinion, based upon well-founded reasons and an understanding of the overall idea, you are well on your way to critical thinking.

Reasoning and Critical Thinking

Imagine a large quilt made up of many small squares. Your first impression may be of its size and its splash of contrasting colors. Your ability to learn with openness makes you take a close look at each square. You study the fine details, the intricate workmanship, and how it was put together to form the overall pattern. With reasoning, you go a step further and place a value on the complete work based on a careful study of the parts. Reasoning is the basis for all critical thinking.

As you step back and look at the quilt after careful examination, you see more than its size and bright colors. You notice more than the elements that make it a worthwhile piece of handiwork. Influenced now by your assessment of the entire quilt, including its smallest details, you form a reasonable opinion of its worth.

The following list describes what is involved in critical thinking. Consider how these possibilities can work for you.

Critical thinking involves . . .

- ❖ understanding.
- ❖ seeing the "big picture."
- ❖ forming a basis for your opinions.
- ❖ determining the significance of something.
- ❖ making decisions.
- ❖ choosing values by a process of reasoning.

Filtering Choices

You operate from a complicated array of influences—mind, emotions, circumstances, resources, and disposition, to name a few. Careful, ordered thinking will make it easier for you to put those influences into perspective, to evaluate options, and to predict their outcomes.

Imagine critical thinking as a kind of filter through which you perceive your choices. The filter affects your viewpoint on everything; it sifts out irrelevant data, allowing you to make choices intelligently. Thoughtfully filtering every choice with critical-thinking strategies will help you to identify your highest values from the knowledge and understanding you have. Using the filter, you will find it easier to prioritize tasks and make sound decisions. Goals will be more reachable as you critically decide for yourself, at every juncture, what your best path to them will be.

Why is this thus? What is the reason for this thusness?

-Artemus Ward

The immediate payoff of critical thinking is elevated academic performance, but it will ultimately reshape your entire future. Life can sometimes seem like an array of random pictures flashing through your mind. If you analyze those pictures, make meaning of them, organize them, and use them in some way, you have begun the critical-thinking process. You will then feel comfortable making rational judgments because you have determined right reasons for your choices and filtered out the wrong ones.

In life situations, a critical thinker can . . .

❖ look intensely at circumstances.
❖ sort events according to significance.
❖ search for options.
❖ choose the best path to follow.

Sometimes all the stored data in your mind seems uselessly strewn about, causing your thoughts to jump from one idea to another with no purpose. This kind of random thinking, often called *daydreaming*, does have a role in learning. It can be used as a springboard for brainstorming, sometimes an effective first step in the critical-thinking process. For example, in writing an essay, you may first jot down a list of creative words that will draw out your imaginative ideas. It is only when you use your critical-thinking abilities to arrange those words into a central theme that your ideas become useful.

Your use of reason can shift your thinking from mere feelings and impressions to valid, knowledge-based reasoning. By thinking critically, the chemistry student can go beyond memorized principles and link them to laboratory procedures and research. Sociology students can use their knowledge of people to make judgments about humanity. Political science majors can study the governments of many countries to gain insights about the world.

Using a Critical-Thinking Plan

Good critical thinkers rarely leave things to chance. First, they become aware of their thought processes and use them to learn on a higher level. Then they create a plan and follow it carefully. In simple terms, they think about thinking. In the academic world, this is called "**metacognition**." If you think about thinking, you will have knowledge about knowledge, and you will know what you know. In this process, you can move from facts to analysis and on to self-assessment—measuring what you know and don't know.

metacognition
a knowledge or awareness of what you know; thinking about thinking

You will enjoy the advantage of having a "map" to figure out the shortest and best way to get from fact to analysis and from information to value judgment. The driver who starts a car and begins to travel with no map or plan in mind will take a long time to get somewhere, and may *never* get there. The critical thinker knows how to reach the destination of conclusions and decisions. From there, a critical thinker will form valid conclusions and act intelligently.

Some people confuse critical-thinking skills with study skills. Both are important, but the two are very different. Study skills usually focus on organization, concentration, and discipline. Critical thinking focuses on weighing and ranking ideas so that links in a chain of argument follow logically. Each link strengthens the total argument.

Filling out the following chart will help you understand better how a critical-thinking plan can be put into practical use. You will need to utilize what you have learned in this chapter, as well as in Chapter 3, to complete the chart. After reading the instructions under each category, use the remaining four rows to fill in information from four of your classes.

Apply reason to your life. Choose a problem, concern, or circumstance you need to change.

Critical-Thinking Plan

Facts

Define your problem. Look
at the facts. Look at your
feelings about them.

_____
_____
_____

Patterns

What is the big picture?
How do the facts and
feelings fit together?

_____
_____
_____

Hypothetical Thinking

What can you change to
make the situation
different? Think of at
least three "What ifs."

_____
_____
_____
_____

Reasons and Implications

Identify reasons to support
each change you thought
about. Identify the
consequences of each
change.

_____
_____
_____
_____
_____

Filter

Eliminate irrelevant facts and
feelings. Eliminate choices
that don't make sense.

_____
_____
_____

**Solutions, Conclusions,
Decisions**

Choose the best option
based upon a set of
reasons you can express.

_____
_____
_____

Apply reason to your class work. Choose a novel or story you are reading for English or a chapter in a history textbook.

Critical-Thinking Plan

Facts
Look at the text carefully. _____
Examine the facts and details. _____

Patterns
Identify the big picture. _____
Search for patterns or _____
related concepts. Categorize _____
the facts. _____

Hypothetical Thinking
In what ways can you explain _____
the big picture? (Think of at _____
least three possible _____
explanations for what's _____
happening.) _____

Reasons and Implications
Think of what each _____
explanation means to the _____
story or chapter. _____

Filter
Eliminate irrelevant facts. _____
Eliminate explanations that _____
don't make sense. _____

Solutions, Conclusions, Decisions
Decide on the best _____
interpretation based upon a _____
set of reasons you can _____
express. _____

Summary

- -

At some time in your life, critical thinking—or the failure to apply it—will change the course of your future. When you have an important decision to make, be ready. You have much to gain by learning to think beyond the facts.

As you think more critically, you will establish values and opinions based on logical reasoning. You will make sound decisions that work for you. Critical thinking affects your viewpoint on everything when you use it as a filter through which to sift your choices.

The benefits of thinking critically are numerous. The following list gives just some of the advantages.

A critical thinker . . .

- ~ goes beyond facts.
- ~ sees the "big picture."
- ~ has a strong basis for opinions.
- ~ finds relationships among ideas.
- ~ determines significance.
- ~ spots weaknesses in other people's reasoning and avoids them in his or her own reasoning.
- ~ challenges flawed arguments.
- ~ chooses values by logical reasoning.
- ~ becomes a wise consumer.
- ~ becomes a discerning voter.
- ~ assesses the ideas of speakers and writers in a variety of situations.

You will not acquire all these benefits merely by chance. As a critical thinker, you must start with a plan—a strategy that begins with a recognition of facts and moves on to patterns and concepts. From there, you explore hypothetical issues and different ways of dealing with the material. Finally, you use reason to reach logical conclusions in order to form judgments, opinions, and values.

Your critical-thinking plan should also include the monitoring of your own comprehension and the measurement of your own learning. Through a process of honest examination, you can recognize what you understand and do not understand—know what you know and admit what you do not know. This is metacognition—knowledge about knowledge.

Let's Talk

1. What is critical thinking? Be specific. Give examples.

2. Explain how critical thinking is like walking away from a microscope and taking a look at the "big picture." Alternately, explain how it is like narrowing your focus from the "big picture" to the microscope's slide.

3. What do you think is more important—studying the details first or taking a look at the "big picture"? Give reasons for your answer.

4. Talk about why it is important to have a critical-thinking plan. Explain your response.

Apply the Concepts

1. In this chapter, you learned about "seeing the big picture" from the example of the quilt and its squares. Write about three other examples where you must first examine the parts to clearly see (understand) the big picture.

2. Critical thinking has been described as a kind of filter through which you perceive things. Using dictionaries, encyclopedias, or other resources, write about three different kinds of filters (air filter, water filter, etc.). Explain how these "filter illustrations" are metaphors for critical thinking.

3. How can you distinguish a good opinion from a bad one? How would you determine if a belief is valid or invalid?

4. Find a current newspaper article in which the writer expresses a strong opinion on something (most newspapers have an "opinion page"). Determine if the author used a relevant critical thinking plan. Be sure to answer questions similar to these: Does the author use facts? Do the facts fit into a pattern? Does the author use reasoning? What weaknesses (or strengths) do you find in the author's reasoning (be specific)? How might you challenge the author's arguments? Be prepared to share your findings with the class.

Part 2

Comprehension Monitoring—
Knowing What You Know

Putting Autonomous Learning to Work

Part One of this course offered you an overall picture of the properties of your mind that make successful thinking possible. By recognizing drive, action, openness, and reason, you discovered qualities that help you use your mind to its full potential. In the process, you've been learning what it takes to be a **self-regulated**, **autonomous** learner.

Wherever Part One has carried you on your intellectual journey, you are no doubt moving closer to a more satisfactory educational experience. You are also setting the stage for success in college and laying the foundation for occupational and personal fulfillment.

Autonomous Learning and You

- -

Although powerful thinking is essential to superior achievement, it seldom stands alone. You will need to examine what goes into making the autonomous learning process work for you. In the high school setting where there is more structure, the teacher often shows you how to complete an assignment. In college, most instructors assume that you are a self-regulated learner—a student who controls your own effort to learn, devises your own study plan, and gets things accomplished on your own. These responsibilities might be difficult for you to assume. This section will ease your way.

self-regulated
controlled or directed by a personally developed plan or method

autonomous
self-governing; self-regulating

A man may die, nations may rise and fall, but an idea lives on.

-John F. Kennedy

The doer alone learneth.

-Friedrich Nietzsche

Begin With Motivation

will
strong sense of purpose or determination

Part Two begins with motivation—having the **will** to apply the four properties of your mind and take control of your learning. Knowing what inspires you to get a job done is the beginning of getting it accomplished. Once you focus your motivation and efforts on well-planned, effective goals, you will enjoy the benefit of increased productivity. Motivation provides the momentum that can put your learning to work for you.

Most people are motivated to work hard on activities they're interested in, like a favorite hobby or favorite class. Next time you're absorbed in your favorite activity, stop for a moment and recognize how much motivation you have. Then notice which properties of the mind you're using to perform well. Remember, your internal motivation and the powerful potential of your mind can be harnessed to bring you success.

Add Your Own Background

Before his name became synonymous with legal thrillers, John Grisham worked 60-70 hours a week as a lawyer in a small Southaven, Mississippi, law firm. He never intended to make writing his career, but his motivation, hard work, education, and life experiences all combined to make him the best-selling novelist of the 1990s.

His experience in criminal defense and the disturbing testimony of a twelve-year-old inspired him to begin his first novel. At 5:00 every morning, he would write for several hours before going off to work. It took him three years to finish that first book, only to see it rejected by many publishers. Persistence paid off. When a publisher finally did accept the manuscript, Grisham was already working on his second novel, *The Firm*, which became an instant best-seller.

Grisham never looked back. He went on to write a novel every year—and to sell the film rights to many of them. He was obviously motivated to write, but he also combined his zeal with knowledge, experience, and hard work to get the job done. Once you harness your inner store of motivation and combine it with all your other experiences, you too will accomplish your goals and realize your dreams.

Techniques That Get the Job Done

- -

In addition to motivation and background, we usually need a plan and some valuable strategies to reach our goals and do things well. Part Two offers you a **repertoire** of techniques that will equip you to get your academic job done now and in college. These same techniques can be easily applied to work and to your favorite hobbies.

repertoire
a set of skills, devices, and techniques used for a particular purpose

Recognizing how you learn and work best, developing your memory, and transforming class notes are three techniques that can elevate your learning and higher-level thinking. True academic competence comes from the realization of what you know—and, even more important, what you don't know. This strategy, called *comprehension monitoring*, lets you check your mastery of the material you are studying. At this level of advanced thinking, you can go beyond the facts, form intelligent opinions, and challenge flawed arguments. All these techniques are part of Part Two's repertoire of skills.

Achievement is Achievable

- -

Advanced thinking makes considerable demands upon the thinker. In the end, however, you will be in control of your academic and personal life. You will realize that achievement, though it comes more easily for some than for others, is achievable through critical thinking and comprehension monitoring.

Just as John Grisham put together all the parts of his life to create success, you will be able to do the same when you finish this course. You will step back and see your education from a different perspective. You will look at it with new values and different opinions. Just as important, you will have the tools—knowledge, strategies, and applications—to be successful.

Chapter

5

MOTIVATED TO ACHIEVE

Motivation—An Internal Resource

External Motivators

False Motivators

Motivation by Value and Interest

Sustaining Your Motivation

Summary

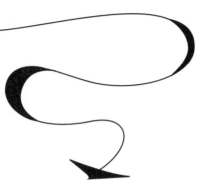

If it is true, as Ralph Waldo Emerson said, that "nothing great was ever achieved without enthusiasm," then motivation must be a component of getting things done. Dictionaries define motivation as "something that causes a person to act." It may be a small inner urge that prompts you to do something small or a lifelong passion that results in the accomplishment of something great. Whatever the result, motivation provides a driving force behind everything you do.

Motivation—An Internal Resource

Getting to school on time every day takes motivation. Ultimately, accomplishing your dreams and goals begins and ends with motivation. Motivation is not something you hope to get or wish you had. It is an internal resource over which you can take firm control.

To a great extent, motivation is influenced by **disposition**. Disposition is not related to what you do, but rather to what you are *inclined* to do. It is not

> Whether you think that you can, or that you can't, you are usually right.
>
> -Henry Ford

disposition
mental outlook or attitude; an inclination or tendency

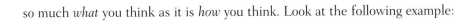

so much *what* you think as it is *how* you think. Look at the following example:

If 50% of a glass has water in it, how do you see the glass?

> *half empty*
> *half full*
> *the wrong size*

If you consider the glass half empty,
you may be disposed to .... **pessimism**

If you think the glass is half full,
you may be disposed to .... **optimism**

If you believe the glass is the wrong size,
you may be disposed to .... **perfectionism**

Fill what's empty, empty what's full, and scratch where it itches.

- Duchess of Windsor, when asked what is the secret of a long and happy life

Whatever your disposition, you can control it, even alter it, in order to improve your motivation and performance.

As a self-regulated, autonomous learner, you are in control of your own learning. Your disposition and motivation are internal and controllable. As you recognize this, you can work to regulate the following important aspects of your learning:

- ~ how you *approach* your tasks—**disposition**
- ~ how you *drive* toward getting them done—**internal motivation**
- ~ how you *do* them—**action**

In a college setting, you need to rely heavily on your ability to control and sustain motivation. College students are responsible for their own learning, as well as for their own personal drive and effort.

Your zeal is invaluable, if a right one.

-Socrates
(from *The Crito*)

DISPOSITION—
how you approach
your task

**INTERNAL
MOTIVATION—**
how you *drive*
your task

ACTION—
how you *do*
your task

External Motivators

- -

Self-motivation may, at times, seem extremely difficult or even impossible. As a result, some people rely heavily on others to motivate them to purposeful action. Highly successful motivators command enormous salaries and sometimes achieve great prominence and impressive results. Many winning athletic coaches are not just good at the game; they are remarkable motivators.

Seminars are crowded with people looking for motivational speakers who will spur them on to action and provide formulas for success. Television is replete with motivators who convince people to buy their products or try their ideas. While there is usually nothing wrong with being encouraged or influenced by a good motivator, it's important to remember that in the end it is your own motivation that must drive your effort; it is only your own effort that produces action.

Some people claim they cannot perform without the encouragement and motivation of another person. Good experiences with interesting teachers, inspiring coaches, or encouraging parents and mentors may have convinced them this is true. But even without an "encourager" or a role model, you have what it takes to trigger motivation and become self-motivated.

False Motivators

Sometimes people find themselves believing in false external motivators over which they have no control. They may depend on circumstances, thinking they are like Cinderella waiting for a "fairy godmother" to arrive instead of devising their own strategies to "get to the ball." Most often, fairy godmothers never arrive.

Take a few moments to review some popularly accepted **fallacies** about success. Think about why these false motivators may not work. Think about how little control you actually have in each situation.

Luck

With just a little bit of luck, I could. . . . How often we believe that luck will someday come our way! What exactly does it mean to be lucky? In most cases, good luck implies that through little or no effort of your own, good fortune will fall into your lap.

Although there is no harm in taking advantage of a lucky situation, you can't count on luck. In reality, most people never win the lottery or become heir to unexpected riches. In fact, counting on luck undermines motivation. A person is left rationalizing—*Why should I work when I might get lucky?*

Luck is the residue of design.
-Branch Rickey
—former owner of the Brooklyn Dodgers

I find that the harder I work, the more luck I seem to have.
-Thomas Jefferson

Other People

Some people claim that parents, coaches, friends, teachers, and others are responsible for properly motivating them. With this mindset, they can blame others for their lack of accomplishment. While influential people sometimes do help us succeed, their influence is not something we can always depend upon.

For instance, one year you may have teachers with whom you are totally in sync. Another year, one teacher may not do what it takes to inspire you to learn. At first, you may label the class boring and the teacher a poor educator. But in reality, you have the power to motivate yourself to learn. Waiting for a teacher to inspire you contradicts the idea of self-motivation.

The choice of your parents, your teacher, and often your coach or boss is out of your control. What you do control is how you perceive your circumstances and how you work with those circumstances. When you have the right disposition, adapting to different people and changing situations will only strengthen your drive and effort.

I once asked my history teacher how we were expected to learn anything useful from his subject, when it seemed to me to be nothing but a monotonous and sordid succession of robber baron scumbags devoid of any admirable human qualities. I failed history.
-Sting
rock musician

Natural Ability

There's no question that natural ability facilitates learning and performance. A high Intelligence Quotient (IQ) makes tasks easier for some students, but IQ is not always an indicator of success. One student with a high IQ may not do as well in school or work as a student with a lower IQ who puts forth more effort.

Even though one student may be talented in music, art, sports, or foreign language, the student with less talent and more determination may do better. It's important to keep in mind that natural talent can be a false motivator if it is not accompanied by effort.

Motivation by Value and Interest

- -

VALUE Perhaps your best internal motivator is **value**. Before you can be genuinely motivated, you need to appreciate the worth or potential importance of an activity. If you discover that something has importance to you, you will be more motivated to work at it.

You may have found it difficult, if not impossible, to find value in some subjects or tasks. First, assume that all courses have some value. Then recognize that value is sometimes obscured or delayed until later. Here are some ways to discover value in your less stimulating classes or assignments.

value
the worth or importance of something

Vague—But Valuable—Motivational Factors

- ~ Pride of accomplishment
- ~ Innate desire to learn
- ~ Sense of achievement
- ~ Competitive spirit
- ~ Fulfillment
- ~ Possible future significance
- ~ Broadening your point of view
- ~ Being able to discuss intelligently

Examine the activities and situations on the following chart to see how recognizing value works. On the left are situations in which the value is easily recognizable. On the right are situations in which you may see no value at first glance. Several areas have been left blank at the end so you can fill in some of your own courses or activities that you may perceive as valueless right now.

VALUE		VALUE	
That is Easy to Recognize		**That is More Difficult to Recognize**	
Activity	**Value**	**Activity**	**Value**
Take a French class	*Situation:* I'm planning to go to France next year as an exchange student. *Value:* I can read and speak French when I'm in France.	Take a French class	*Situation:* I want to be a computer programmer. Why take French? *Value:* Computers are worldwide—I may do business with French speakers.
Take a health class	*Situation:* I'm an athlete. *Value:* I need to know how my body works and how to keep it healthy.	Take a health class	*Situation:* I'm a music major. Why take health? *Value:* It's a required course for graduation.
Take an English composition class	*Situation:* I want to become a journalist. *Value:* To be a good journalist, I need to know how to write well.	Take an English composition class	*Situation:* I'll be studying auto mechanics at technical college. English doesn't apply to this career. *Value:* Someday, I may use good writing skills in other aspects of my life.
My activity or task: _____ _____ _____ _____	What is its value? _____ _____ _____ _____	My activity or task: _____ _____ _____ _____	What is its value? _____ _____ _____ _____
My activity or task: _____ _____ _____ _____	What is its value? _____ _____ _____ _____	My activity or task: _____ _____ _____ _____	What is its value? _____ _____ _____ _____

Most of the time, motivation comes naturally when you recognize the value and worth of your task. In the past, you may have given up on a difficult or uninteresting class. Perhaps you dropped a course or suffered through it, receiving a less-than-satisfactory grade.

No doubt, the situation would have been different if you had broadened your perspective or recognized some obvious or even some obscure factors for motivation. Keep in mind that motivation can also be based upon the fact that the course is required. That is a valid motivation.

INTEREST Valuing something alone does not ensure action. You accomplish things when you have enough interest in what you value to do something with it. For example, you may value an activity like visiting the elderly because you know it is worthwhile. But unless you are interested enough to go see them, your value will have no effect.

The same principle applies to your education. You may value a college degree and realize it's what you need to accomplish your goals. However, unless you are interested enough in it to do what it takes to graduate from college, your belief in its value will be ineffective. You control what you value, and you determine the result of what you consider important.

Sustaining Your Motivation

Some may think, *I've set goals before and never reached them.* Others may argue, *I always start out a new school year with lots of enthusiasm, but something happens after a month or two to make me lose interest.* If you've had thoughts like these, you may have suffered from what is called a lack of sustained motivation.

Generating enthusiasm for something new, different, and exciting is usually rather easy. Maintaining that enthusiasm over the long course, however, takes effort. Motivation can be sustained, or even recovered, by understanding how to "keep the juices flowing."

Self-motivation starts with the belief that you are in control of your own get-up-and-go and, in fact, that you want to get up and go. Then you need to believe that you can do what you must do to get the job done. Finally you need to know how to stay motivated to accomplish your goals.

A man will fight harder for his interests than for his rights.

-Napoleon Bonaparte

Do, or do not. There is no "try."

-Yoda
The Empire Strikes Back

Each year, more than a million students drop out of school.

One out of four students who start college fails to finish.

Since self-esteem may be a key to your motivation, remember always to "write a winning script" for your life and for every goal you have. The following "winning script" for sustaining motivation may give you some ideas for maintaining your own high level of personal determination.

A "Winning Script" for Sustained Motivation

Beliefs

~ I believe my efforts make the difference between success and failure.

~ I believe it's my responsibility, not my teacher's or anyone else's, to make sure I do well.

~ I believe that working smart, not just being smart, leads to top performance.

~ I care about what I do.

~ I believe I can find what is interesting in a boring class.

~ I will keep my goals in mind.

Actions

~ I will attribute my successes and failures to my own effort (or lack of it), not just luck.

~ I will separate the subject from the teacher. Then I will focus on the best qualities of each class or situation and try to work around their less-positive qualities.

~ I will put forth the effort to do the course work.

~ I will find extra time for what I value.

~ I will search for interesting information (e.g., on the Internet) about a boring class.

I will ask at least one relevant question during each class session. At the end of each class, I will recall at least one piece of interesting information.

I will think of several ways the subject might be useful. I will consider how I might use this subject in everyday living.

~ I will break down long-term goals into dozens, or even hundreds, of short-term goals.

I will allow for failures and try again.

Summary

Everything we do begins with some degree of motivation. Menial tasks, as well as lifelong goals, require motivation. Working with your own disposition, you can control and improve your motivation and achieve your goals. External motivators can be beneficial in helping you accomplish purposeful action. Teachers, coaches, parents, speakers, friends, and others may, at times, spur you on to achievement, but true motivation is always internal. Even without an "encourager," you have what it takes to be self-motivated. Self-motivation depends on the genuine belief that your own efforts—not false motivators like luck, other people, or natural talent—will make the greatest difference.

Probably the best internal motivator combines that belief in the effectiveness of your effort with a strong sense of the value, or worth, of an activity. Although some activities or courses may have obvious value, others may not. When uninteresting activities shut down your motivation, you need to search for less-obvious motivational factors like pride of accomplishment or possible future usefulness.

Usually motivation comes naturally when you find and recognize value. Taking enough interest in what you attach importance to will then ensure action and results. Remember that you determine the outcome of those efforts you consider important.

Let's Talk

1. Write your own definition of motivation.

2. What does the following statement mean to you? *Motivation is an internal resource over which I have control.*

3. How is motivation influenced by disposition? How does your disposition affect your motivation?

4. When have external motivators been beneficial to you? Give specific examples. When have external motivators been detrimental to you? Give specific examples.

Apply the Concepts

1. Explain how you can still "write a winning script for your life" when you're surrounded by tough circumstances.

2. Write about your life as if it were a movie. Although your story line will have conflicts and crises, be sure you have a positive, winning conclusion.

3. Which of the following false motivators do you rely on most (or have you relied on most in the past)—luck, other people, or natural ability? Explain in detail how this false motivator is an ineffective means for accomplishing your goals.

4. If value is, in fact, a primary motivator, then how do you go about finding it in an activity you consider of low value? Give examples.

5. Describe a class or assignment you presently find uninteresting or useless. Explain why your motivation is low for this class or activity. Then explore what value it has (see examples of values that are more difficult to recognize on page 57). You may need to search for vague (but valuable) motivational factors (see page 56). Identify one way this class or assignment could be useful to you in the future.

6. Write a short essay about a social issue that you value (for example, visiting the elderly, ending world hunger, helping the homeless, stopping drunk driving, etc.). Explain why you value this issue. Then tell about your involvement in the issue (what you've done to make it happen). How might you increase your level of involvement in this issue (what more can you do with your value)?

Chapter

6

Setting Effective Goals

In the previous chapter, you saw how action is generated by motivation and effort. But many of us don't know where to concentrate our efforts. We often try to do so many things that nothing ever seems to get done.

Henry David Thoreau seemed to have the answer to this dilemma. He said, "In the long run men hit only what they aim at."

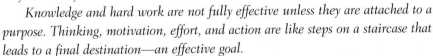

Knowledge and hard work are not fully effective unless they are attached to a purpose. Thinking, motivation, effort, and action are like steps on a staircase that leads to a final destination—an effective goal.

It's important to keep in mind that goals can be set in all aspects of your life—academic, social, personal, and occupational—and the same thinking process applies no matter what kind of goal you are setting. Every worthwhile endeavor begins with a worthwhile goal. You may spend many years of your life in school, but unless your education is focused on an end result—like establishing the career of your choice—your efforts will not produce tangible rewards. The solution then is basic: (1) know how to set effective goals; (2) know how to prioritize them; and (3) know how to accomplish them.

Most of us have too many goals, and we assign them all equal value. We shift focus from one goal to another, thereby increasing the sense of being out of control.

-Dr. Joyce Brothers

Obstacles are those frightful things you see when you take your eyes off your goal.

-Henry Ford

Four Key Elements of an Effective Goal

- -

Goals are usually achieved by successfully completing a logical progression of short-term goals. In other words, you can finish a big job by identifying and accomplishing the small jobs that will get it done. No longer will you need to worry about a huge assignment. It will be challenging, but it will also be completely attainable.

The following Four Key Elements of an Effective Goal will help you determine how to establish and recognize effective, reachable goals.

FOUR KEY ELEMENTS OF AN EFFECTIVE GOAL

 ### Specific and Measurable

A specific, measurable goal describes what you want to accomplish with as much detail as possible and in terms you can clearly evaluate.

Poor: *I want to earn a lot of money this summer.*

Better: *I want to earn at least $100 per week this summer as a caddie.*

 ### Challenging

To accomplish a challenging goal you must have energy and discipline.

Poor: *I want to make it to all my classes tomorrow.*

Better: *I want to have perfect attendance in all my classes for the next six weeks.*

 ### Realistic

A realistic goal is one you are capable of obtaining.

Poor: *I want to be elected Student Association President in my first semester of college.*

Better: *I want to run for Student Association office by my junior year of college.*

 ### Small Enough to Be Completed by a Certain Date

Often it is necessary to break long-term goals into short-term goals with clearly specified completion dates.

Poor: *I want to see the world before I die.*

Better: *I want to visit Mexico City by next spring.*

Goals Should Be Specific and Measurable For a goal to be effective, it must be *specific*—fully and clearly expressed without vagueness, leaving no question as to meaning or intent.

> **Vague goal:** *I want to be a great success.*
> **Specific goal:** *I want to be a successful trial attorney.*

An effective goal must also be *measurable*—it must tell exactly how you will know when you have accomplished it.

> **Unmeasurable Goal:** *I want to be a successful trial attorney.*
> **Measurable Goal:** *After working as a trial lawyer for five years, I want to have a 75% success rate.*

SOCIAL GOALS Setting specific, measurable goals also applies to your social life. For example, suppose you made the following goal:

> *I want to improve my social life.*

This goal is not specific or measurable because it is vague and has varying meanings. To one person, improve your social life might mean talking on the phone longer every day. To another person, improve your social life might mean getting a whole new group of friends. The following goal is better since it is detailed and assessable:

> *I want to improve my social life by making two new friends by next Saturday.*

With this exact goal in mind, you will know what to do to achieve your goal. You will also know, by next Saturday, if you have achieved what you set out to do.

ACADEMIC GOALS Now apply the "specific" and "measurable" criteria to academic goals, to school assignments. Specific, measurable goals also apply to daily school assignments. As a rule, college coursework consists of an assignment and a due date. Seldom will anyone walk you through the necessary steps to complete the assignment. That is why you need to set your own academic goals. Suppose your college history course syllabus lists a test on Chapters 3–10 for a week from Friday.

If you merely made the test your goal, the task would be unclear and perhaps overwhelming. But if you were to break down the assignment into several clear-cut, smaller goals, it might read like this:

> You got to be careful if you don't know where you're going, because you might not get there.
>
> -Yogi Berra

This Friday: *Confirm with instructor that test is next Friday.*
Monday: *Review Chapters 3-6*
Tuesday: *Review Chapters 7-10*
Wednesday: *Study lecture notes and review questions at the end of each chapter*
Thursday: *Get together with a classmate to quiz each other on the material*

Knowing precisely what you have to do is often enough motivation to get the job done. Many people fail to complete assignments or complete a task because they haven't thought through exactly what they need to do. As a result, they often do nothing.

2 Goals Should Be Challenging If your goal is not challenging, it really cannot be considered a goal. By definition, a goal is something toward which effort is directed. The key word here is *effort*—there is effort, and thus challenge, involved in every goal. Your goal may be to improve your game of tennis, but if you don't make an effort to run faster for the tough shots, your game will not get any better.

The ultimate measure of a man is not where he stands in moments of comfort, but where he stands at times of challenge and controversy.

-Martin Luther King, Jr.

When you set goals, the end must take you further than you have already come. For instance, let's say you have typically received a grade of B in your science classes. If your goal for chemistry were to receive at least a B for the semester, you would not have a challenging goal. A challenging goal, on the other hand, would be to receive an A in chemistry for the semester.

3 Goals Should Be Realistic An effective goal must take effort, but what if it is so challenging that it is unreachable? Many goals prove ineffective because they are not realistic. For example, your goal may be to finish a four-year college course in three years. If you will also need to work at least 25 hours a week to pay for your education, your goal may turn out to be unattainable. As you balance challenge with common sense, you will set realistic goals.

It's kind of fun to do the impossible.

-Walt Disney

4 Goals Should Be Small Enough to Be Completed by a Certain Date

At times, a goal may seem so large that you doubt you will ever accomplish it by the deadline. On the other hand, if you feel you have forever to get a big job done, you may find it difficult to get started. Before you write off an assignment as unattainable or procrastinate your work into nonexistence, try breaking down a job into a series of smaller tasks that can be completed by assigned dates.

If you know when a task needs to be done, you are more likely to use your time wisely to meet your goal. As you set short-term goals and give them deadlines, you will need to schedule them so you can easily meet your long-term goal.

Goal-setting does not apply only to school work. It can be the secret to managing your life. In almost any of life's situations, you can set several, a dozen, or even a hundred, manageable short-term goals to reach a long-term goal.

Below are examples of long-term goals that have been broken down into short-term goals with deadlines. The short-term goals begin at the bottom and work their way progressively up the steps to the long-term goal at the top. As you review these examples, think about your own goals and how they might fit into these patterns.

> Life is what happens while you're busy making other plans.
>
> –John Lennon

Academic Goal

Attend College in Fall After High School Graduation

Apply to college by fall of senior year.

By the beginning of my senior year, choose a college best suited to my area of interest

During my junior year, research at least three colleges I may want to attend.

Take the SAT or ACT in spring of my junior year.

Have a counselor evaluate my high school program now.

Occupational Goal

Become a Certified Engineer by the Age of 25

Apply to engineering colleges by the middle of my senior year.

Check my high school courses against the college admissions requirements so I can alter my schedule before my junior year begins.

Research admissions requirements at three engineering colleges before my junior year

Take several advanced high school math classes

Social Goal

Travel to Spain with My Friends After Graduation

Purchase plane ticket and raise remainder of money at least one month before departure.

Get necessary shots, visa, passport, etc. at least one month before departure.

Find out how much the trip will cost. Put away $250 for trip deposit by January of my senior year.

Practice Spanish with Travel Club members during my senior year.

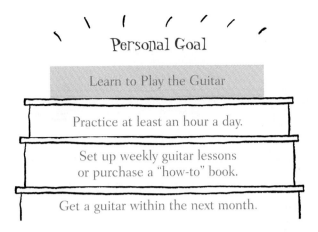

Personal Goal

Learn to Play the Guitar

Practice at least an hour a day.

Set up weekly guitar lessons
or purchase a "how-to" book.

Get a guitar within the next month.

Now take some time to set your own goals on the blank staircases that follow. First, put your long-term goal on the top step. Then, starting with the bottom step, fill in the short-term goals that will get you to the top. Your short-term goals should be in logical, chronological progression and have practical completion dates.

Academic Goal

6

5

4

3

2

1

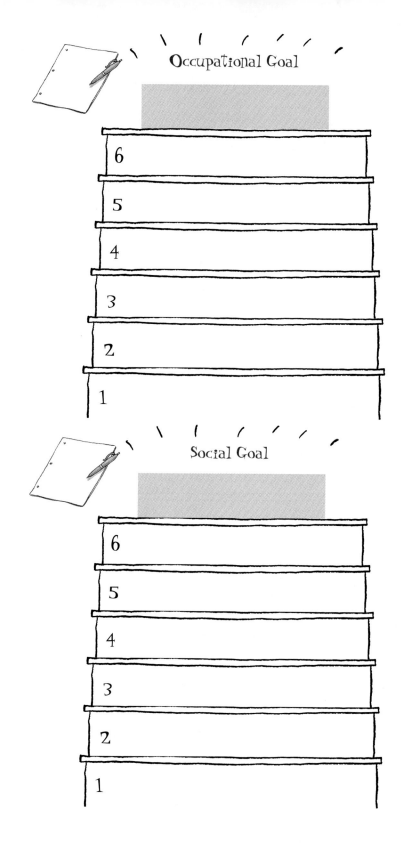

Personal Goal

6

5

4

3

2

1

Time and Task Management

Once you've set effective goals and broken them down into short-term tasks, it's time to make a plan for achieving them. Successful students find that assignments and responsibilities do not overwhelm them when they effectively manage their time and their tasks within an existing timeframe. Time cannot be managed, but tasks can.

It's not uncommon to walk through a college dining hall and hear students discussing their tough schedules and their inability to get everything done. In reality, time is rarely the real problem. Managing time is often just a matter of realizing how much time there is in a week. Notice how the following graph breaks down a typical 168-hour week.

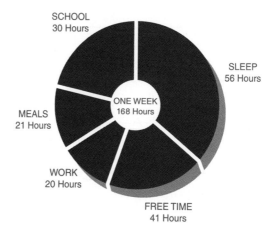

SCHOOL
30 Hours

SLEEP
56 Hours

ONE WEEK
168 Hours

MEALS
21 Hours

WORK
20 Hours

FREE TIME
41 Hours

As the graph shows, there are more free-time hours in a week than any other activity except sleep. Time itself is usually not the issue. Most often, what you really need to get your work done on time is quality of effort and effective task management.

Successful learners and workers think in terms of task rather than time. If you depend only upon a time orientation, you may create a schedule that looks ideal but falls short of your expectations.

For instance, one evening you may set aside two hours for a history assignment. At the end of the two hours, you may be disappointed that you have not accomplished very much. You may have sat diligently for the time allotted, but daydreams, distractions, and unexpected challenges thwarted your plan.

In contrast, a student who is task oriented defines the task and then breaks it down into short, doable units—ten minutes here, twenty minutes there. You complete one small task at a time until the entire job is done. By breaking down the large task into smaller ones, you can keep producing and, at the same time, allow yourself adequate relief through short breaks.

Without realizing it, most people already manage their time and their tasks in many areas of their lives. Nearly everyone routinely breaks down larger goals into smaller, manageable tasks every day. For instance, think of what you have to accomplish just to go to a movie with a friend.

Let's go to a movie!

Start here

Find out what's playing

Decide which showing you want to attend.

Get some money.

Invite some friends to go with you.

Arrange for transportation.

Get to the movie on time!

This kind of task management comes naturally, so managing your school assignments should also come naturally if you use the same principles. In the following task management exercise, break down one of your larger assignments into smaller tasks. Assign short timeframes to each task.

Large Assignment: _____

Start here to break down your large assignment into smaller tasks.

1. _____ (___ min.)

2. _____ (___ min.)

3. _____ (___ min.)   5. _____ (___ min.)

4. _____ (___ min.)

A plan like this for every major assignment will boost your productivity. Being productive in college is harder than being productive in high school. Rarely does anyone at college remind you to get started on a task or tell you how to complete it. Most college instructors assign huge projects—term papers, oral presentations, mid-term exams, final exams—without breaking them down into realistic parts. You alone will be responsible for setting up a task management plan and then sticking to it.

Multitasking

Breaking down a task into small, manageable parts is an effective learning strategy, but your plan may be sabotaged when you suddenly have five things to do at once. A task management plan called multitasking can be applied to several simultaneous tasks. Look at the following multitasking problem that is typical of those you may face in college.

[1] Lamott, Anne. *Bird by Bird: Some Instructions on Writing and Life.* 1994. Pantheon Books, Random House.

Multitasking Problem

You are taking 17 credit hours: ~ psychology 101   ~ history
                                 ~ introduction to   ~ English
                                   biology   composition
                                                       ~ chemistry

Psych has a thousand terms to learn; you hate biology because you can't keep all the facts straight; you think history is okay, but you have a term paper hanging over your head; for English you have to write a short paper every week; and in chemistry, even if you understand the chapter as you read it, by the time you get to the end, you are confused and don't know which formulas to use for the homework exercises.

This week you have: ~   an exam in biology (you haven't read the chapter yet)

~   homework due in chemistry (no credit for late work)

~   a paper for English

~   a test in history

~   a huge chapter to read in psychology

Where Should You Start?

1. Identify your tasks—everything you need to do to get your work done in every subject.

2. Make sure to list your tasks in small parts.

3. Allot a time for each small task (5, 10, 15, or 20 minutes). (REMEMBER: You do not need to do all parts of one subject at the same time; doing small tasks and resting or going to something else makes the assignments much less tiring.)

4. Check off ☑ completed tasks as you finish them.

The Result

You will find that you have enough time during the week to finish your tasks. You may discover that you have some time left over. The secret is multitasking, managing several tasks at once. Each small task takes you closer to your goals. Several large assignments that once seemed overwhelming become a manageable series of smaller, realistic tasks.

Using the Task Management Plan below, practice multitasking by developing a plan to complete your own assignments that are due in the next week or so.

Task Management Plan (Multitasking Strategy)

The courses I am taking: ~ _____
~ _____
~ _____
~ _____
~ _____

My assignments for the next week or so:

#1 _____
#2 _____
#3 _____
#4 _____
#5 _____

**My Assignments Broken Down Into Small Tasks
(5, 10, 15, or 20 minutes each):**

#1 ☐ _____ (____ min.) ☐ _____ (____ min.)
☐ _____ (____ min.) ☐ _____ (____ min.)
#2 ☐ _____ (____ min.) ☐ _____ (____ min.)
☐ _____ (____ min.) ☐ _____ (____ min.)
#3 ☐ _____ (____ min.) ☐ _____ (____ min.)
☐ _____ (____ min.) ☐ _____ (____ min.)
#4 ☐ _____ (____ min.) ☐ _____ (____ min.)
☐ _____ (____ min.) ☐ _____ (____ min.)
#5 ☐ _____ (____ min.) ☐ _____ (____ min.)
☐ _____ (____ min.) ☐ _____ (____ min.)

Check off ☑ completed tasks as you finish them.

Another effective technique for multitasking is putting your tasks on a calendar. Using the situation below, create a multitasking plan. First, put the assignments on the appropriate days. Then break them down into smaller tasks and put those tasks on the calendar. Remember to assign short timeframes to each task.

The Situation

Today is Tuesday. Your family is having company for dinner tonight, and they want your presence and your help. You have 50 pages of reading and a reaction paper due on Thursday for your English class. An oral presentation in your business class is due on Friday. A week from today, you have a math exam. Put the big assignments on the calendar first. Then break them down into smaller tasks with due dates and put those tasks on the calendar. How well did you manage your tasks and your time?

Multitasking Calendar

SUN	MON	TUES	WED	THURS	FRI	SAT
		(TODAY) Guests for dinner (attend and help)				

Multitasking strategies can easily be compared to the multitasking capabilities of a computer. Just as a computer can simultaneously run multiple programs (an Internet browser, spreadsheets, publishing programs, word-processing programs, calculating functions), so your mind is able to manage multiple tasks. You will have the ability to move from assignment to assignment and from task to task when your plan is in order.

Setting Priorities

Although a computer can run more than one program at a time, the computer operator works only on one thing at a time. The person at the computer may be generating a report on a word-processing program, inserting information from a spreadsheet and the Internet, and using the calculator for formulas. The focus of the person, however, is on just one thing—the report.

So it is with the human brain. It is capable of handling many functions, but action is directed at one task at a time. Choosing which task to work on at the moment is called *setting priorities*.

When you have conflicting demands on your time, it helps to evaluate each task in terms of *urgency, visibility,* and *weight*. This helps you concentrate on the most critical or valuable tasks and put aside less-important tasks until later. You may find you can eliminate some tasks entirely when you realize that they have little effect on your life.

When determining priorities, ask yourself questions like the ones in the following boxes. Your answers should make it clear which assignment or job you should tackle first, second, or third. It will also help you determine which tasks can die without consequence.

Urgency
(Questions for Determining Priorities)

1. What will happen if I don't complete this task right now? _____

   _____

   _____

   _____

   (Example: An assignment is due tomorrow. Your teacher gives no credit for late work. If you don't do it now and turn it in on time, you won't receive any credit for it.)

2. What if I don't complete this task at all? _____

   _____

   _____

   _____

   (Example: Sometimes it makes no difference if you complete a task or not. If your task is to write in your journal for your own enjoyment, then you can get rid of this task if you need to.)

3. What is at stake if I don't do this task now? (a) my grade
   (b) a relationship (c) my happiness (d) other (explain): _____

   _____

   _____

   _____

   (Hint: Always think about the consequences of not doing a task before you decide not to do it.)

4. How will I affect other people by not doing this task right away? ___

   _____

   _____

   _____

   (Example: If five other people can't begin their work until I finish mine, this task has more urgency.)

Visibility
(Questions for Determining Priorities)

1. Who asked me to perform this task? _____
   Who will notice if I don't do it first or don't do it well? _____
   (*Remember: A small task requested by a high-ranking person, i.e. your boss or your teacher, may take precedence over a larger task requested by someone at a lower level.*)

2. Is this task something that will be noticed by a larger group of people, or will it only affect me? _____
   (*Example: If you're preparing a speech to present to the City Council about why the city should donate computers to your school, then your work may be noticed by the whole city.*)

Weight
(Questions for Determining Priorities)

1. How much time will this task take? _____
   (*Example: If your task is small, you may want to do it right away to eliminate something quickly from your to-do list. However, if you work better when the longer, more complex task is completed, then you may want to work on it first.*)

2. What is the importance of this one task to my future? _____
   _____
   (*Note: To answer this question, you will have to look at the big picture. For example, if your task is filling out an application for college, then you need to determine if handing it in late will affect your ability to go to college. A task should take high priority if it could affect your future a great deal.*)

EXERCISE IN PRIORITIZING SEVERAL TASKS Think of a situation you are facing now (or have faced in the past) in which several tasks need to be done at the same time. These can be a combination of tasks from school, work, home, or any other situation. Make a list of at least five things that you need to do.

To use the following chart, list your five tasks at the top. Answer the questions about each task for each of the categories listed in the left-hand column. You may have to go back to the boxes on *urgency, visibility,* and *weight* above to answer some of the questions.

After analyzing your responses, assign each task a number from one through five (one being the top-priority task, five being the lowest-priority task, and so on).

Priority-Setting Chart

Task 1: _____

Task 2: _____

Task 3: _____

Task 4: _____

Task 5: _____

	Task 1	Task 2	Task 3	Task 4	Task 5
What's at stake if not done now? (Urgency)					
Who will notice if task not done now? (Visibility)					
How much time will task take? (Time)					
What will happen if I don't do the task? (Consequence)					
What is the importance of this task to the future? (Weight)					
PRIORITY (Rank) 1= extremely important 5 = not at all important					

Now take the same chart below and list the same five tasks again at the top. This time, give the chart to a classmate to fill out. Your classmate may have to ask you some questions about your tasks.

After your classmate has filled out your chart, compare it to the one you completed for yourself. What are the differences? Would you change your priorities in any way, based on your classmate's input? Why or why not?

Sometimes, someone else's perspective will help you examine your own priorities in a different way.

Priority-Setting Chart

Task 1: _____

Task 2: _____

Task 3: _____

Task 4: _____

Task 5: _____

	Task 1	Task 2	Task 3	Task 4	Task 5
What's at stake if not done now? (Urgency)					
Who will notice if task not done now? (Visibility)					
How much time will task take? (Time)					
What will happen if I don't do the task? (Consequence)					
What is the importance of this task to the future? (Weight)					
PRIORITY (Rank) 1 = extremely important 5 = not at all important					

Summary

Setting effective goals can change the course of your life. Instead of just having a lot of knowledge and aimlessly putting forth a lot of undirected motivation and effort, you can accomplish things you never thought possible. Goals that once seemed unachievable become a series of practical, doable, short-term tasks. A challenging goal is no longer an excuse for defeat; it is an opportunity to accomplish things you've never done before.

> Nothing comes from nothing.
> -William Shakespeare

Once you're focused on attainable goals, you can make your plan to achieve them by successful time and task management. Since time is rarely the problem, you will need to improve your quality of effort and optimize your task orientation.

Once you realize how you naturally manage tasks in your everyday activities, you will be able to transfer those abilities to your academic, social, and personal responsibilities. Breaking down a huge job into smaller tasks is the first step. Then you will be ready to take on more than one assignment or responsibility at a time through multitasking strategies.

When too many tasks overwhelm you, it's helpful to evaluate each responsibility in terms of urgency, visibility, and weight. By prioritizing your tasks, you will know their order of importance and where you should focus your efforts first. You may also learn that some tasks can be completely eliminated. Overall, you will be well on your way to successfully completing your goals and assignments.

Let's Talk

1. What are two challenging goals that you have for your life? How do you plan to accomplish these goals? Detail the steps you will take. What elements of an effective goal (page 64) are present in your plans?

2. What are the benefits of breaking down a goal into smaller tasks?

3. Why should you have a deadline for your goals and tasks?

4. What do you think produces more effective results—time management or task management? Explain in detail.

5. Why is setting task priorities an essential ingredient of effective multitasking?

Apply the Concepts

1. For one week, keep a "task diary." Enter all of the tasks you need to do and their deadlines. Cross out the completed tasks as you go along and note how long each took to accomplish. At the end of the week, examine your productivity. (How did you do with task management, multitasking, and setting priorities? Did you break down large assignments into smaller, doable tasks? Were your time estimates accurate?) Now give yourself a productivity grade (A, B, C, D, F). Explain why your productivity for the week deserves that grade. Explain how you can improve your "grade."

2. What area of your life do you usually place first on your priority list? (a) family (b) friends (c) school work (d) social life (e) job (f) other: _____. When is it *not* beneficial to make this your top priority?

3. Make a list of all the tasks you need to get done this week. Include all sources like school, home, work, social life, etc. Strike through those you can eliminate without consequence. Rank the remaining tasks with a 1, 2, or 3 (1 = high priority; 2 = medium priority; 3 = low priority). Beside each task, jot down what the consequence will be if it is left undone.

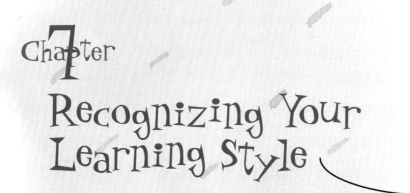

Chapter 7
Recognizing Your Learning Style

Your Study Preferences and How You Learn Best

Your Learning Style and the Right Brain/Left Brain Theory

Learning Styles and Gardner's Intelligences

Summary

By now, you may be feeling highly motivated with a sense of accomplishment as you complete your assignments through a series of smaller, progressive tasks. Now, exploring your own learning style and discovering how you learn best can bring you even further along in your quest for overall achievement.

In this chapter, you will find three different ways to look at your personal study preferences and learning styles. You will realize the advantage of tailoring your learning and your study habits to your unique style. At the same time, you will discover that learning situations do not always match your style. You will see why you need to be competent in other learning styles and adapt to them when necessary.

As you investigate how you learn best, you will no doubt learn many things about yourself and the environment in which you live. Understanding your learning style starts with knowing who you are—the person you are deep inside, not who you would like to be or feel you ought to be.

The higher up you go, the more mistakes you are allowed. Right at the top, if you make enough of them, it's considered to be your style.

-Fred Astaire

Your Study Preferences and How You Learn Best

Paying attention to how and when you learn best will no doubt elevate your performance and trim your study time. Being aware of your study preferences may also give you strong hints about your future life's work. Just as you gravitate toward a learning style you enjoy, so will you gravitate toward vocations that are in sync with who you are and how you enjoy working.

Answering the following questions will help you get started thinking about how you prefer to learn.

~ What are my study strengths (organization, hard work, etc.)? _____

_____

_____

~ What are my study weaknesses (unorganized, easily distracted, etc.)? ___

_____

_____

~ Under what circumstances do I study best? _____

_____

_____

~ What kind of learning gets me excited? _____

_____

_____

~ What motivates me to do an assignment? _____

_____

_____

~ How did I study for the last test on which I did particularly well? _____

_____

_____

Now take a look at your specific study preferences.

Study Preferences

Physical When I study, I like to:

- ❏ sit in one place
- ❏ move around
- ❏ study in the morning
- ❏ study in the afternoon
- ❏ study in the evening
- ❏ eat
- ❏ refrain from eating
- ❏ sit up straight
- ❏ lie down or slouch

Environmental When I study, I prefer:

- ❏ a quiet room
- ❏ music playing
- ❏ people around
- ❏ dim lighting
- ❏ bright lighting
- ❏ natural sunlight
- ❏ a cool room
- ❏ a warm room
- ❏ outdoors
- ❏ a desk
- ❏ a couch
- ❏ a bed
- ❏ the floor
- ❏ a tree

Social When I study, I like to:

- ❏ work by myself
- ❏ work with one other person
- ❏ work on a team
- ❏ ask questions
- ❏ find out the answers myself
- ❏ get feedback from adults (teachers, parents, etc.)
- ❏ use self-feedback (ask myself questions)
- ❏ talk about the material to someone else
- ❏ keep what I'm learning to myself

Personal When I study, I like to:

- ❏ work on short assignments
- ❏ work on big projects
- ❏ work in several short time segments
- ❏ work for long stretches of time on one thing
- ❏ be self-motivated
- ❏ have someone spur me on
- ❏ have someone make me do it, now
- ❏ make long-range plans
- ❏ make short-term plans
- ❏ not make plans at all

There are many benefits to recognizing how you study best. Some of them are listed below. You will probably realize many more as you fashion your studies, and eventually your career, to fit your preferences whenever possible.

Benefits of Studying in Your Preferred Style

~ You save time by studying the easiest and most natural way.

~ You enjoy studying more.

~ You understand why you sometimes have trouble studying in other circumstances.

~ You can create comfortable shortcuts to achievement.

~ You can choose a career that matches your style.

LEARNING AGAINST THE GRAIN Sometimes learning within your own style is not possible. If you study best in a dimly lit room, then brightly lit classrooms will go against your grain. If you need a quiet environment and the band is practicing in the room next to your study hall, frustration may set in.

When you have a teacher who is detail-oriented and you learn better with broad ideas and creativity, you may not do as well in that class. These seemingly hostile circumstances could give you an excuse for not completing your work, or they could present a valuable opportunity to experience learning as a kind of resistance training.

Athletes know the value of working on weaknesses in order to build stronger, more-skilled bodies. So it is with learning. Adapting to less than comfortable learning conditions can often strengthen your ability to achieve rather than weaken it.

Sometimes learning "against the grain" feels almost impossible. Learning in uncomfortable ways, or ways you aren't used to, can cause you to resist, and often retreat from, learning. Doing an actual, "against-the-grain" exercise will help to illustrate this point.

"Against-the-Grain" Exercise

Exercise: *On the lines below, sign your name with the hand you're not used to writing with. Do it several times.*

_____ _____

_____ _____

How does your signature look to you? _____

How closely does it resemble your real signature? _____

Could it use some improvement? _____

How did this exercise make you feel? _____

How did you feel physically (especially your hand and fingers)? _____

How do you feel about practicing this until your signature is equally good with both hands? _____

_____

If you were asked to perfect the opposite-hand signature, you might resist the tedious work involved in such a task. But what if there were a significant reward for accomplishing that feat? Suppose your teacher offered $1,000, an "A" for the term, or a college scholarship to anyone in the class who could sign his or her name equally well with both hands by the end of next week. Suddenly, resistance would seem a foolish option.

When the reward is attractive enough, most people will work against their grain to get a job done. So it is with academic learning situations. Working in ways contrary to your own comfortable learning style takes added motivation and harder work. However, the reward—the end result—can be worth it.

Keep in mind that your learning style is nothing more than a preference. You may prefer orange juice in the morning, but you would probably drink cranberry juice instead, if you had to. You may prefer to sit in the back of a movie theater, but if the only seats available are in the first three rows, and you really want to see the movie, you would probably sit up front.

No matter how different your learning situation is from your ideal, you do not need to abandon the assignment or the task. You merely have to make some adjustments to get it accomplished.

> The reward for a thing well done is to have done it.
>
> -Ralph Waldo Emerson

> If people are good only because they fear punishment, and hope for reward, then we are a sorry lot indeed.
>
> -Albert Einstein

Your Learning Style and the Right Brain/Left Brain Theory

You've seen how personal learning preferences can differ from person to person. In addition, people can process information in diverse ways. Perhaps you've attended a movie with a friend and talked about it afterward. You may have been surprised that your friend perceived the movie in a completely different way than you did. It may seem almost as if you saw different movies. While your friend saw all the little details you hardly noticed, you saw the development of the overall theme that your friend barely grasped. Why? It could be that one of you is inclined to think more with the left side of the brain while the other is using more of the right side.

Studies and experimentation have demonstrated that the two different hemispheres of the brain are responsible for different modes of thinking. The result of these studies is a left brain/right brain theory. This theory suggests that (a) different sides of the brain control different ways of thinking; and (b) that most people are inclined to use one side more than the other.

Scientists have long known that different spheres of the brain govern different **cognitive** functions. In the 1960s and 1970s, however, educators began to examine how the left brain/right brain theory pertains to student learning. They found that most students are predisposed to using one side more than the other. On the other hand, some students are "whole brained," equally adept at both approaches to thinking. The following chart gives an overall view of right brain/left brain thinking.

The right half of the brain controls the left half of the body. This means that only left handed people are in their right mind.

-Anonymous

cognitive
relating to or involving the process of thinking and knowing

Left Brain

Analytic

Logical
Capable of reasoning or of using reason in an orderly, rational manner

Sequential
Examines things in an orderly succession or arrangement to gain understanding

Analyzes
Studies the parts of something to determine their true nature or relationships to each other

Objective
Deals with facts as perceived without distorting them with personal feelings, prejudices, or interpretations

Right Brain

Global

Random
Without a definite plan; without regard for regularity or pattern

Intuitive
Gains knowledge or understanding by quick and ready insight

Synthesizes
Combines diverse concepts into a coherent whole, often forming a new, complex idea

Subjective
Perceives things as affected by personal views, experience, or background

Looks at the Parts

Analytic
Masters the small parts of a problem before looking at the big picture; often not concerned with the overview

Looks at the Whole

Global
Sees the big picture; often not concerned with details

To find out if you are more inclined to think with your left brain (analytic), your right brain (global), or equally with both (whole brain), try the following exercise. Circle all the words that describe you.

free with feelings	adapts to reality
connections important; a lumper	fact-oriented
playful	one project at a time
distinctions important; a splitter	imaginative
orderly, systematic	detailed; sees the parts
controls feelings	several projects at a time
responds to verbal instructions	likes open-ended questions
thinks with words; sentences	people-oriented
fluid; spontaneous	linear
creates reality	likes multiple-choice tests
thinks with images, pictures	likes stories, anecdotes
serious worker	time-focused
rational; logical	no sense of time
risk taker	holistic; sees the big picture

Now look at the same descriptions below, sorted according to left-brain/right-brain characteristics.

Left-Brain

adapts to reality

fact-oriented

one project at a time

distinctions important; a splitter

orderly, systematic

responds to verbal instructions

thinks with words; sentences

linear

likes multiple-choice tests

controls feelings

serious worker

time-focused

rational; logical

detailed; sees the parts

Number circled _____

Right Brain

free with feelings

connections important; a lumper

playful

imaginative

several projects at a time

likes open-ended questions

people-oriented

fluid; spontaneous

creates reality

thinks with images, pictures

likes stories, anecdotes

no sense of time

risk taker

holistic; sees the big picture

Number circled _____

Add up the number of descriptions you circled in each column. The column with the higher number is an indication of your left-brained or right-brained preference. The further apart the two numbers are, the more inclined you are to think dominantly in one mode. If the numbers are equal or close to it, you may be more "whole-brained."

Remember that successful people may be left-brained, right-brained, or whole-brained. Some professions, however, seem to attract analytic thinkers (accounting, research, computer programming), while others attract those who think globally (art, music, politics, teaching, acting).

Knowing your left-brain/right-brain inclinations will probably help you learn better and help you make life choices that fit your style. Although you will need to adapt to many situations that are contrary to your style, life will be easier and more enjoyable if you learn, live, and work in an environment where your inclinations are not frustrated. When you can, do your hard jobs at the time and in the way that best suits your learning preference.

In general, schools tend to favor left-brained learning with a focus on facts, definitions, and accuracy. If you are more right-brained—predisposed to aesthetics, feelings, and creativity—you may find it more difficult to utilize your learning style in traditional educational settings. However, with some resourcefulness, you can supplement analysis, calculation, and reading with patterns, metaphors, analogies, role-playing, and visuals to make your educational experiences fit your style. Never stop when assignments don't suit you. Be flexible and be creative. In your later college years, you will be rewarded for your global preferences.

Below is a visual array of left-brain and right-brain characteristics. See how many you can correctly label as left-brain or right-brain. (The correct answers are found at the end of this chapter.)

> For I am a bear of very little brain and long words bother me.
>
> -A.A. Milne
> *Winnie the Pooh* author

1.   **2.**

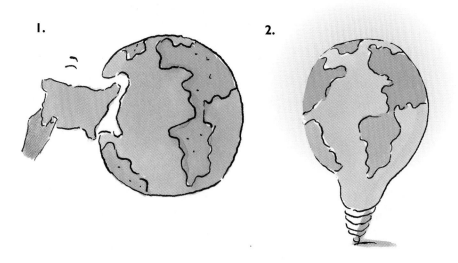

3.

4.

5.

6.

7.

IT'D BETTER BE EXACTLY 5 POUNDS.

8.

Learning Styles and Gardner's Intelligences

Recognizing your own learning style also involves knowing how your own mind and distinctive talents affect the way you learn. Start by asking yourself, *When do I feel smart?* This doesn't mean that you need to evaluate yourself on the basis of IQ, ACT/SAT tests, or grades. It means to identify how you process information with the most success. You might ask yourself, *In what context do I learn and function at my fullest capacity with the greatest personal satisfaction?*

WHO'S SMART? Howard Gardner of Harvard University began his analysis of learning preferences by asking this question: *Who's smart?* He was concerned that schools measured "smartness" by giving a general test (often the IQ test). He criticized this method of gauging intelligence because it focused basically on language and math/science skills. He claimed that IQ tests manage to survive only because they seem to value what is valued by schools—language, math, and science.

Gardner identified several human intelligences characterized by what he called a pattern of neurological organization and a unique cluster of abilities. He described intelligence as "an ability to solve a problem or fashion a product that is valued in at least one culture or community.":[1] In short, Gardner's study emphasized the complexity of individual differences and abilities. He showed that students learn most successfully when they have opportunities to use their unique talents to process information.

The following table will give you an overview of the intelligences that Gardner has identified, along with the professions that a person with each is likely to be attracted to. As you consider each intelligence, note which may be dominant for you.

[1] Gardner, Howard, Lecture, Cambridge, MA, Summer, 1996.

Music is the art of thinking with sounds.

—Jules Combarieu

Gardner's Intelligences

Intelligence	Definition	Likely Profession
Verbal/Linguistic	Relates to a person's ability to learn by responding to words. People who are "language smart" learn well through expressive language. They are likely to enjoy reading, writing, and speaking.	journalist writer, editor newscaster, announcer speaker, politician
Logical-Mathematical	Relates to people who can recognize symbols and patterns and understand their relationships. People who are "logical-mathematical smart" are good with numbers, reasoning, logic, problem solving, patterns, and abstract thought.	scientist, mathematician computer programmer, accountant, banker, researcher, teacher (math, science, economy), some philosophers
Musical	Relates to people who perceive, remember, and express themselves through sound, rhythm, and pitch. People who are "music smart" use music as a primary way of knowing. Music is a means of expression and an avenue for processing information.	composer, musician conductor, music therapist music teacher, sound engineer film director/producer
Visual-Spatial	Relates to people who think best through visual perceptions and mental representations. People who are "spatial smart" create mental pictures and three-dimensional concepts to help them understand. They are keenly aware of shapes and three-dimensional images. They like maps, charts, tables, graphs, and puzzles.	sculptor, artist, architect, engineer, interior designer, graphic designer, inventor, sailor
Bodily-Kinesthetic	Relates to people who use movement as a way of understanding. People who are "bodily-kinesthetic smart" associate thought with motion. They need to move to know, often moving objects around to understand concepts. They learn through a "hands-on" approach, preferring to participate rather than just watch.	athlete, dancer, actor/actress, mechanic, artist, surgeon
Interpersonal	Relates to people who use their awareness of other people as a basis for action. People who are "interpersonal smart" get along well with others and are sensitive to what others think and feel. They openly exchange thoughts with others and participate in group activities.	teacher, salesperson, politician religious leader, motivational speaker, counselor
Intrapersonal	Relates to people who use an awareness of their own thoughts and feelings to guide their behavior. People who are "intrapersonal smart" don't need others to affirm their ideas or encourage them. They are intuitive, self-motivated, content to be by themselves.	researcher, writer, psychiatrist, counselor, motivational speaker
Naturalist	Relates to people who recognize patterns in the world, especially the way plants grow and animals behave, and understand details of the environment. People who are "naturalist smart" are in tune with the natural cycles of nature.	farmer, forest ranger, meteorologist, geologist, botanist, ecologist

It is important to remember that most people have *all* of these intelligences to some extent. Most people, however, find it easier to process information with their dominant intelligence(s). Once you know how you are "smart," you will be able to build upon it and give yourself opportunities to learn in comfortable, effective ways.

As you gain confidence in your intelligence(s), you may discover that you are "smart" in other contexts. For example, Michael Jordan initially succeeded in basketball due to his bodily-kinesthetic intelligence. Later, he found that he had great interpersonal intelligence, which became the foundation for many of his other activities, including advertising and team ownership.

ADAPTING LEARNING TO YOUR INTELLIGENCE Think of yourself now in terms of Gardner's intelligences. Go back to the list of intelligences and determine your strongest intelligence. Then rank your next two or three intelligences in order of their dominance.

Now relate your strongest intelligence to your school assignments. Many assignments may adapt well to your dominant intelligence. For instance, if you are an athlete (bodily-kinesthetic), try using your workouts as a way to memorize vocabulary or study for a history test. Your workout rhythms can become a framework for key words you need to recall. If you are musically smart, try putting definitions or terms to a tune or a rhythm.

In addition to developing your strong intelligence(s), be sure to also develop your weaker intelligence(s) by connecting them to your strengths. In other words, if you are not particularly logical-mathematical, don't completely avoid analysis and hypothesis in your studies. Associate some deductive thinking and abstract thought with your dominant intelligence.

Below is an example of one educational concept (Boyle's Law) and how it applies to all of Gardner's intelligences.

There is nothing more notable in Socrates than that he found time, when he was an old man, to learn music and dancing, and thought it time well spent.

-Michel de Montaigne

Boyle's Law

For a fixed mass and temperature of gas, the pressure is inversely proportional to the volume.

Objective: To teach the concept of Boyle's Law

Students are provided with a verbal definition of Boyle's Law and discuss the definition. (*Linguistic Intelligence*)

Students are given a formula that describes Boyle's Law, and they solve specific problems connected to it. ($P \times V = K$; e.g. a pressure (P) of atm $\times$ a Volume of 5 cubic centimeters = a constant (K) of 10.) (*Logical-Mathematical Intelligence*)

Students are given a metaphor or visual image for Boyle's Law. ("Imagine that you have a boil on your hand that you start to squeeze. As you squeeze it, the pressure builds. The more you squeeze, the tighter the pressure, until it finally bursts and pus goes spurting all over the room.") (*Spatial Intelligence*)

Students do an experiment breathing air into their mouths so that their cheeks puff up slightly. Then they put all the air into one side of their mouth (less volume) and indicate whether pressure goes up or down on that side (it goes up). They are asked to release the air into both sides of their mouth (more volume) and indicate whether pressure has gone up or down (it goes down). (*Bodily-Kinesthetic Intelligence*)

Students rhythmically repeat a musical mnemonic (something intended to aid memory). (*Musical Intelligence*)

> When the volume goes down,
> The pressure goes up;
> The blood starts to boil
> And a scream erupts,
> "I need more space
> Or I'm going to frown."
> The volume goes up
> And the pressure goes down.

Students become "molecules" of air in a "container" (a clearly defined corner of the classroom). They move at a constant rate (temperature) and cannot leave the container (constant mass). Gradually, the container is reduced in size as two volunteers holding a piece of yarn representing one side of the container start moving it in on the "people molecules." The smaller the space, the more pressure (e.g. bumping into each other) is observed; the greater the space, the less pressure there is. (*Interpersonal Intelligence; Bodily-Kinesthetic Intelligence*)

Students are asked to measure the differences in indoor and outdoor air pressure. (*Naturalist Intelligence*)

Students are asked about times in their lives when they were "under pressure"—"Did you feel like you had a lot of space?" (Typical answer: lots of pressure—not much space). Students are then asked about times when they felt little pressure (little pressure—lots of space). Experiences are related to Boyle's Law. (*Intrapersonal Intelligence*)

Summary

Understanding your own study preferences enhances your ability to learn well. By recognizing your physical, environmental, social, and personal preferences, you will be able to fashion your study habits to reflect the way you learn best and adapt to less than comfortable situations.

Since people process information in different ways, it is helpful to recognize learning style as it relates to thinking with your left brain, right brain, or whole brain. Whether you are left-brained (analytic) or right-brained (global), your thinking affects your performance. Knowing your left-brain/right-brain inclination will help you learn and work in situations that fit your way of thinking. Strengthening the weaker hemisphere of your brain will elevate achievement in your more difficult subjects.

A study of Howard Gardner's intelligences shows you the complexities of individual differences and abilities and how they affect the way you learn. Whether you are linguistic or spatial, musical or bodily-kinesthetic, your dominant intelligence will most likely provide opportunities for you to learn in comfortable ways. As you make complete use of your dominant intelligence, you will gain confidence in your unique way of learning. You will also find yourself able to build up your less-dominant intelligences and connect them to your strengths.

Let's Talk

1. How are surroundings (environment) important for successful learning? Describe an uncomfortable learning environment for you. How would you adapt to it? Be specific.

2. Describe an assignment you've had that definitely went "against your grain." Explain in detail how it did not match your learning style. Discuss ways you could have adapted it to your preferred way of learning.

3. Are you more left-brained (analytic) or right-brained (global)? Explain what characteristics make you more inclined to that particular way of thinking.

4. Which one of Gardner's intelligences do you perceive as your strongest intelligence? Explain how you know. What are your other strong intelligences?

Apply the Concepts

1. Keep a log for a week, briefly detailing your study sessions. Keep a record of where you study, how you study, how long you study, the environment in which you study, and your distractions. At the end of the week, write about (a) any patterns you perceive, and (b) which study sessions produced the best results (explain why).

2. Draw a rough sketch of your favorite place to study. Label each item as (a) performance enhancer, (b) distraction, or (c) neutral. Write about how you might adjust your study area to achieve maximum performance. If your area is already perfect, explain why.

3. On the continuum below, plot the extent to which you think you are left-brained (put an "L" on that spot of the continuum). Do the same thing for the extent to which you think you are right-brained (put an "R" on that spot). Under what circumstances does the less-used side of your brain become dominant? Why do you think this happens? Be specific.

| Not at all | At times | Half the time | Frequently | All the time |

4. Suppose you are predominantly left-brained. What specific challenges do you anticipate facing in college? Now suppose you are predominantly right-brained. What different kind of challenges do you anticipate in college? Be specific and give examples.

5. Suppose a student with strong linguistic intelligence is struggling with a required course in algebra. Describe at least three ways this student could use linguistic intelligence to learn a logical discipline like algebra.

6. Using Gardner's intelligences, identify your most dominant intelligence. What academic course or subject area do you struggle with most? Explain in detail how you could put your dominant intelligence to work for you to do well in that course or subject.

(Answers to left-brain/right brain exercise on pages 96-97: 1. Left 2. Right 3. Right 4. Left 5. Left 6. Right 7. Left 8. Right)

Chapter

8

UNDERSTANDING MEMORY

It would be hard to imagine life without memory. Our memories tell us who we are, where we've been, and who has accompanied us on our lifelong journey. We use our memories in many different ways: some memories let us drive a car or play baseball without having to learn how to brake or catch each time. Some memories let us follow familiar procedures such as using a calculator or brushing our teeth. Other memories call back incidents in our lives. These memories add up to our experience, and it is experience that helps us respond to new situations. But the memories that are most likely to help us grow socially and intellectually are those that we create in the process of learning.

All that we learn gets stored in our memories, ready to be retrieved when the information is called for. Thinking skills demand that we call upon those memories to make meaning of new information. We use our memories to create new memories and make meaning of the combination of old and new memories. The more we remember, the richer our lives.

The Memory Process

Although sophisticated medical technology can pinpoint the location of memory in the brain, any knowledge we have of the way memory works depends solely upon human observation and analysis. Without knowing much about the brain itself, we can know that learning directly involves our ability to remember.

Researchers have found that the brain has three different stages of processing information—*acquisition, retention,* and *retrieval.* The pathway from acquisition to retention in learning takes human effort. Retention is the point at which you make information your own—where you choose to save what you have learned for possible future use.

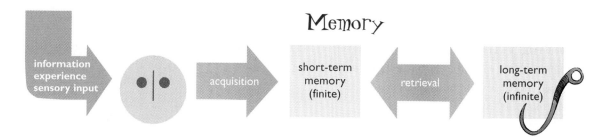

Acquisition

Through the acquisition process the brain gets information. Hundreds of pieces of information flow into your brain every minute. You receive this information through your five senses—sight, smell, hearing, taste, and touch. This information is called *sensory input*. Because there are so many choices, your brain takes in only what you pay attention to.

The more you consciously respond to what your senses offer, the more you remember. In other words, the more you pay attention to what you see, smell, hear, taste, and touch, the more you will be able to remember and use the information those senses provide.

Take your sense of hearing, for example. You may listen to a class lecture, but if you're not paying close attention—not keenly tuned-in or interested— the information will surely get lost.

> The art of true memory is the art of attention.
>
> -Samuel Johnson

If, on the other hand, you hear an interesting conversation in the hall between classes, you might find yourself moving a little closer, listening harder, and even trying a little lip-reading if it gets too noisy. Because the topic interests you, you acquire the information. For at least a short time you can remember every word. Essentially, you have to care about what you are going to remember.

Retention

Retention and memory are basically the same thing. What you retain, you remember. How long you retain information depends upon how you process it. First information goes into your short-term memory, a brief storage system. You temporarily park information there for a short period of time. It is much like placing documents on the desktop of your computer until you decide whether to store them permanently or delete them.

Some say that short-term memory lasts only seconds; others say it may last as long as a day or so. In any event, memory often seems to be fleeting and to have a limited capacity.

Maybe you've had the experience of looking up a phone number, only to forget it by the time you walk across the room. Or maybe you've stood blankly in a room wondering what you had just reminded yourself to do seconds before. That's short-term memory.

To retain information, you must purposefully move the material from your short-term to your long-term memory. Your short-term memory's capacity is simply too limited to store a lot of information. True retention, or learning, lies in your long-term memory, which has infinite capacity. If you want to remember something for a long time, you must decide to place it permanently into long-term storage. If you are careful how you put material there, you will find it is easier to get it out when you need it. In the complex process of retention—making sure the information "sticks"—you need to do several things:

> Memory is a net. One finds it full of fish when he takes it from the brook, but a dozen miles of water have run through it without sticking.
>
> -Oliver Wendell Holmes

Getting Information to "Stick"

1. Impose order on the information.
2. Relate the information to what you already know.
3. Reorganize information into logical patterns.
4. Provide a "hook" to fish out the information you need.
5. Review the information with its "hook."

IMPOSING ORDER ON INFORMATION If you allow bits of information to enter your brain randomly, piece by piece, you will probably have a difficult time retrieving them when you want to. On the other hand, if you impose some sort of order on incoming data, you will be more apt to find them later.

As you organize data in long-term memory storage, you are actually creating **mental hooks** or **mnemonic** strategies to help you with information retrieval. Creating mental hooks is like making folders and directories on your computer hard drive.

Scattering hundreds of files haphazardly on your computer desktop makes it difficult for you to find them when you need them. However, when you lump similar files together into categories and place them in a folder with a clearly defined label, retrieval is easy. A mental hook is a clearly labeled folder in your mind that will help you find things later.

An organized brain also helps you form concepts and patterns more easily. It helps you relate new, incoming information to data you've stored there in the past. A well-ordered memory is prepared to pull up relevant data needed for interpreting, reasoning, and judging.

REVIEWING WHAT YOU KNOW No matter how carefully you put information into your memory, you won't be able to use it unless you can retrieve it. Retrieval of retained information in the long run depends upon reinforcement. Planned review reinforces newly retained information and keeps it available for use. Studies show a high rate of forgetting when there is no review of information.

mental hook
a memory strategy used to impose order on information in order to improve retrieval

mnemonic
intended to help memory

If you hear a lecture, you will probably forget about 75% of it by the next day. Within about a week, you will remember almost nothing about the lecture. However, experiments show that with just ten minutes of daily review, a person will remember well over 75% of a lecture at the end of one week, and still about 75% at the end of four weeks.

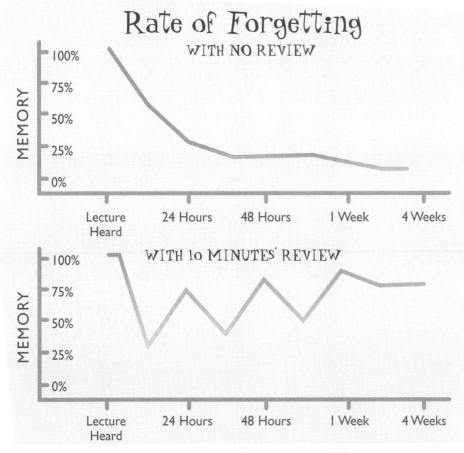

It is important to note that you can only remember what is meaningful to you. As you process new material, you must connect it to something you already know. Sometimes this process can distort what's coming in. (Stereotypes, prejudice, preconceived ideas, your own experience—all can change what you remember.) If you are careful, however, you can adjust for these distortions, but keep in mind that memory is *always* in part constructed by what you know and how you process the incoming information.

Retrieval

Feeding your brain lots of information is admirable, but if you can't retrieve data when you need them, your jam-packed memory won't serve much purpose. Retrieving information—bringing stored data out of your memory for some purpose—is the end result of learning. Retrieval makes learning useful and applicable.

As a student, you probably think of retrieval mostly in terms of test situations where you search your mind for facts reviewed the night before. Sometimes you are sure the answer is somewhere in long-term storage, but you can't seem to pull it out. That's when you need to use a memory hook.

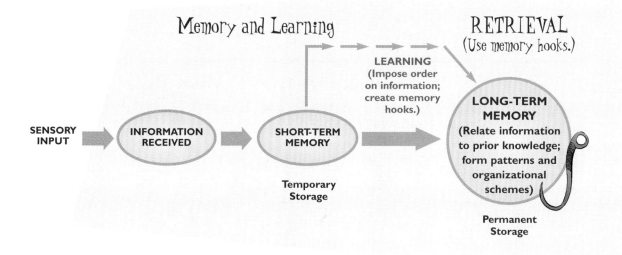

Memory Hooks Following are several different types of memory hooks that may be useful to you as you practice efficient memory retention and retrieval.

KEY WORDS Particularly effective memory hooks that you have probably used all of your life are *key words*. "Key" words literally "unlock" your memory by providing a familiar retrieval cue. Actors often use the first word of a line to trigger the recall of several lines. Some lawyers use one important word to call up the facts of an entire case that they may need as a legal precedent.

You probably use key words when you jot down class notes.

Using the right key word on an Internet search engine will result in productive retrieval of information. In the same way, strategic key words will initiate a powerful search of your mind.

As you use key words in your studies, remember that they are *triggers* or *pathways* that help your mind connect with the actual information. They are not complete answers.

> A student was given an assignment to write a paragraph about cooking. She wanted to write about "monkfish," something she had eaten many years ago, but she could never remember the name of the fish.
>
> She recalled that the fish had something to do with the "clergy" (the key word she used to store the experience in her long-term memory). She considered priest-fish, deacon-fish, preacher-fish, rabbi-fish. Finally, hooking into her memory, using a key word association, she recalled *monk*fish. She knew immediately that was correct.

Key words are valuable because of their amazing versatility. They trigger a range of associations. Here's an example:

1 A key word may stimulate your memory to recall **comprehensive** information.

   Example: *In a course on post-World War II history, some key words might be "Cold War," "NATO," "Marshall Plan," or "British Commonwealth."*

comprehensive
broad in scope or content

2 A key word may capture a **concept** rather than data.

   Example: *Key words in a philosophy course might be "free will," "fatalism," "determinism," and "predestination."*

concept
a general notion or idea

3 A key word or phrase may be purely **associative**.

   Example: *The key words "phone home" from the movie E.T. conjure up both the circumstances and the emotions of the extraterrestrial.*

associative
resulting from relating a mixture of facts, conclusions, and judgments to each other

The following information provides some helpful ways to apply key words to your school work.

KEY WORD APPLICATIONS

NOTE TAKING Highlight or underline key words that bring to mind (a) comprehensive information, (b) concepts, or (c) possible test questions.

GRAPHIC REPRESENTATIONS: Graphic representations give an overall picture of related data. Graphics work like key words to trigger your memory. (Example: Instead of trying to memorize a list of percentage statistics, make a pie graph. The image will remind you of the statistics.)

TEXTBOOK READING: While reading your textbook, highlight or underline key words that give answers to the questions that text headings and subheadings suggest. Where the text has no headings, circle key words that might serve as headings and then highlight the words that support them. (If you can't write in your text, try making a glossary of key words in your notebook.)

CHUNKING Another effective memory hook is chunking. When you chunk information, you group data together into a category, organizing them so that the group identity or function is apparent.

Suppose you had to know the following terms for biology class:

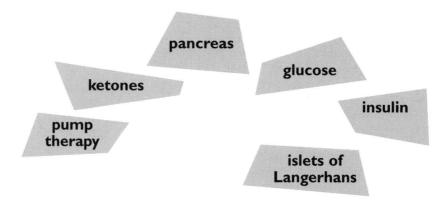

Storing them in your memory, one by one, would cause memory retrieval problems. If you were to chunk them, however, into a category—**Diabetes**—you would be able to retrieve all six words at once and immediately give them organization and identity. With only one hook from your memory. you can recall all six terms.

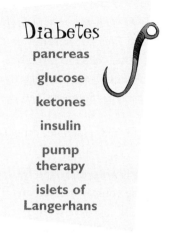

Diabetes
pancreas
glucose
ketones
insulin
pump
therapy
islets of
Langerhans

RHYMES AND SONGS Rhymes and songs also provide good memory hooks. Do you remember how you learned which months have 30 days, which have 31, and the exception with 28 and sometimes 29? It was a rhyme.

Thirty days hath September, April, June, and November . . .

Linking information to a song or tune is especially helpful for students with a dominant musical intelligence. Many people first learned their alphabet by singing it.

A, B, C, D, E, F, G . . .

STORIES Stories are very helpful in stimulating memory. If your teacher tells a story while making a key point, use the story as a hook to retrieve that point. You may even have your own relevant story to tuck into your memory as a hook.

Storytelling is common to all cultures; for many years, history was held only in the memories of storytellers.

Our children's children will hear a good story.

-Richard Adams
Watership Down

VISUALIZING The ancient Greek philosopher Aristotle suggested remembering items on a list just by placing them mentally in a familiar place. He recommended that you take your list, walk around a familiar room, and mentally deposit each item in a different spot. Let's apply this to the diabetes example mentioned above.

> To remember the terms for diabetes, walk through your bedroom and mentally place **insulin** on your bed. Then put **ketones** on the dresser, hang the **islets of Langerhans** in the closet, tape the **pancreas** to the mirror, and so on. When you need to recall these terms, mentally take a walk through your bedroom and retrieve the items from your bed, your dresser, your closet, etc.

This type of hook works for many people, especially those with strong visual-spatial intelligence.

ACRONYMS An acronym is a word formed by using the first letters of several words or phrases. Creating your own acronyms from lists of facts will help you recall them as a unit. If you have a leftover letter in your acronym when you retrieve information, you will know you're missing a fact. That leftover letter will also provide you with another hook—the first letter of the word you're trying to remember.

> Think of the word **HOMES** to remember the five great lakes—**H**uron, **O**ntario, **M**ichigan, **E**rie, and **S**uperior.

You may have your own way of creating a hook to retrieve information from your memory. Whatever you use, remember that hooks may be the only way you ever retrieve some information, and hooks will save you valuable time.

I hear and I forget. I see and I remember. I do and I understand.

-Confucius

Summary

As far as we know, the human mind has an unlimited capacity for stored information. Having room to store everything that goes into your brain is not the problem. The difficulty lies in the ability to retain information and retrieve it when you need it.

When your brain acquires data through the senses, some bits of information are kept in short-term memory for a brief period of time. Other information is sent to long-term storage with meaningful cues or hooks. (Some cues are conscious; others stem from the experience itself.)

When you consciously decide to place something in permanent memory, you give it meaning or impose some order on it. You relate it to what you already know, fitting it into patterns and organizational schemes. The more order you place on acquired information, and the more you review it, the easier it will be for you to retrieve it later.

Making sure that you will be able to retrieve information as needed depends to a large extent on your strategic use of mental hooks. Rather than store data at random, you will find that organizing them into categories will make them more easily accessible. A strategic hook will be the method, the trigger, or the pathway you use to find information and quickly make use of it.

Some particularly effective hooks include key words, chunking, rhymes and songs, stories, visualizing, and acronyms. You may come up with other hooks that work well for you. Whatever your method, retrieval is the essential end result.

1. What is your earliest memory? Why do you think it embedded itself so firmly in your mind?

2. Look at the three stages of memory—acquisition, retention, retrieval. Explain what would happen if any one of them were eliminated.

3. What do you think is meant by "paying close attention"? How does paying attention affect (or not affect) memory retention?

4. Do you think it is possible to retain information without effort? Explain why or why not.

5. At what point in the memory process does learning take place? Do you consider information "learned" if it remains in your short-term memory for a brief period of time? Explain your answer.

Apply the Concepts

1. Briefly jot down what you remember from your favorite class today. Then jot down what you remember from your least favorite class today. Is there a difference in the quantity and quality of what you remember from class? Explain any differences.

2. Create an acronym, a rhyme, or a song that will serve as a "hook" to remember something you are presently studying.

3. Sit by yourself in the lunchroom or another crowded place. Be aware of how you are acquiring information through your senses (especially hearing, smell, and sight). Notice what makes your attention shift from one stimulus to another. Briefly describe why the shift happens.

4. Try out at least three types of mental hooks in some of your classes this week (choose from key words, chunking, visualizing, acronyms, stories, rhymes and songs, or some of your own). Keep a list of the hooks you used and how you used them. Then next to each hook, explain how the technique helped you remember course material more efficiently. (If the hook did not help you, note that also.) Explain which type of hook was most effective for you and why.

MASTERING COURSE MATERIAL

In a perfect world, you would have no problem being motivated to do everything you needed to. You would also be able to remember everything you saw and heard, recalling it and using it at will. In a classroom situation, you would read the course material, understand its concepts, and recall it whenever necessary.

Unfortunately, it's not a perfect world, and you have to work hard to master vast amounts of information. Effective use of critical thinking techniques, however, can help you assimilate course material with greater ease and more understanding. These techniques will also help you confirm what you really know, without being fooled by an *illusion* of understanding.

We often think we know something because we can repeat a memorized list of definitions or recite the proper dates for a string of historical events. When we're asked on a test to show what relationship those events have to each other, however, we're often stumped. Thinking critically through your course material will eliminate this illusion of knowing.

illusion
something that deceives or misleads your mind

Levels of Questions

- -

Games lubricate the body
and the mind.

-Benjamin Franklin

Judge a man by his
questions rather than by
his answers.

-Voltaire

Real knowledge of your course material can come from being skilled at self-questioning. Imagine all the information that you cover in a course as the "answers." Your part is to come up with the right questions to elicit those answers.

In this chapter, you will learn how to ask yourself four different levels of questions that will help you master course material. The questions are progressive—they start by pointing just to the *facts* and then move on to questions that deal with *concepts*, *hypotheses*, and finally *opinions*. As you ask questions about your notes and reading material, you'll see how you are actually preparing yourself to think critically. As you confirm your understanding, you prepare yourself to use the filter of reason and develop new ideas.

FOUR LEVELS OF QUESTIONS Now let's take a close look at the four levels of questions. The examples show how they can be used in a history course, but you can adapt them to master the material in any of your courses.

fact
something that can be
proven

**I have six honest serving
men; they taught me all I
knew. Their names are
what and why and when
and how and where and
who.**

-Rudyard Kipling

LEVEL 1 QUESTIONS
Questions That Point to *Fact*

KEY WORDS:
- who
- what
- where
- when
- why (if verifiable)

EXAMPLE: After reading a chapter on the Civil War, write down questions that the text answers. These questions must point to verifiable facts.

- **Who** *was the general for the South?*
- **What** *were General Meade's battle strategies?*
- **Where** *did the war begin?*
- **When** *was the Emancipation Proclamation issued?*

REMEMBER: In most courses, you can't get away from learning facts—definitions, dates, places, events. The answer to a Level 1 Question is always a fact that can be proven. There is no opportunity for interpretation or judgment in this level of learning.

LEVEL 2 QUESTIONS

Questions That Use Facts to Form *Concepts*

(These questions give *meaning* to data in Level 1)

concept
a general idea connecting
related specifics

KEY WORDS:

- describe/discuss   • compare/contrast   • agree/disagree
- solve   • organize   • relate
- define function (what something does)

EXAMPLE: After taking notes on a lecture about the Civil War, write down questions that the lecture answers. These questions must form relationships and develop concepts from verifiable facts.

> *How do General Lee's battle strategies **compare** with the battle strategies of General Meade?*

REMEMBER: Level 2 questions cause you to explore more complex issues than do Level 1 questions. Level 2 questions put data into particular concepts or ideas. Facts take on meaning when you see them in terms of a comparison, a relationship, a solution, a structure, a function, or a problem to be solved.

Each problem that I solved became a rule which served afterwards to solve other problems.

-Rene Descartes

LEVEL 3 QUESTIONS

Questions That Form a *Hypothesis*

(These questions can only be built on
an understanding of Levels 1 and 2)

KEY WORDS:

- What if...?
- options

EXAMPLE: Next week you will be taking an essay test on the Civil War unit. As you study for the test, ask questions about your notes and reading that will create different perspectives on the facts.

What if Lee had prevailed? How would Reconstruction following the Civil War have been different?

REMEMBER: This is the level at which innovative thought takes place, where judgments are made. Here you have the opportunity to contribute to a new or different interpretation of the facts. You can experiment with hypothetical situations and establish the groundwork for your own viewpoints.

This level works especially well for science courses—*If hot doesn't work, perhaps I should try cold. Would the liquid pour faster or slower if I altered its temperature?*

The test of a first-rate intelligence is the ability to hold two opposed ideas in mind at the same time and still retain the ability to function.

-F. Scott Fitzgerald

LEVEL 4 QUESTIONS

Questions That Call for *Judgment, Choice, or Opinion*

(These questions are based on
what the facts mean to you personally)

KEY WORDS:

- believe
- prefer
- rank
- value
- choose

EXAMPLE: You have chosen the Civil War as a broad topic for your research paper. The following question will be the basis for your thesis statement:

*Did the Civil War have a positive or a
negative permanent impact on American history?*

REMEMBER: Forming judgments and opinions makes you delve into your own preferences and ask how you rank or value data. Opinions and judgments are never simple. They always initially involve your mastery of the first three levels of questions—facts, concepts, and hypotheses. Ultimately, you must identify your options. Then, and only then, can you make a wise judgment or form a well-founded opinion.

> It is the mark of an educated mind to be able to entertain a thought without accepting it.
>
> —Aristotle

QUESTIONS IN DIFFERENT DISCIPLINES Higher-level questions take different forms in different **disciplines**. One strategy used by successful learners involves recognizing those differences in course content. Specifically, you must identify the unique questions and methodology of the discipline. Consider the following example as it might be studied in different fields.

discipline
a field of instruction or learning

Questions in Different Disciplines

Dr. Smith is preparing to do an experiment. There are three beakers on the table: two full and one empty. The room has three tables in it (including the one in front of Dr. Smith), a sink, a desk, a chair, four stools, and numerous items of lab equipment. Dr. Smith is the head of research at this institution and is excited about the upcoming results.

Different disciplines will explore different elements in this situation. Consider four levels of questions in each discipline:

Chemistry: What solution is in each beaker? (Level 1)
Compare the chemical compositions of the solutions. (Level 2)
What reactions would occur if the solutions were mixed? (Level 3)
How important will this finding be to the future of chemistry? (Level 4)

Physics: What is the density of each solution?
Discuss the effect of density on the rate of travel of a liquid.
Would the liquid pour faster or slower if its temperature were altered?
How might study of fluid dynamics influence Dr. Smith's research methods?

Philosophy: What is it that Dr. Smith wants to achieve?
Discuss the ethical issues raised by this experiment.
What would be the ethical implications if Dr. Smith chose to administer
    the solution to animals?
Do you think the experiment is ethical? Why?

English: What is the form of a research proposal?
Describe the style elements of a research proposal.
What would be the effect if some of these elements were altered?
Evaluate the quality of the research proposal.

Accounting: How much do the materials cost?
Do a cost-benefits analysis of Dr. Smith's experiment.
What if Dr. Smith used less-expensive materials?
Rank the importance of different elements of the experiment taking cost
    into account. Should any costs be eliminated?

History: During what time period is Dr. Smith doing the experiment?
Compare Dr. Smith's work to the work of others in the field during that time.
What if Dr. Smith never did this experiment?
Why is such research important for the development of society?

Mathematics: What is the volume of the solutions in the beakers?
Describe how to calculate the volume of a three-dimensional solid.
What would the percent increase in volume be if the beakers' heights were doubled?
Rank order the three most important mathematical findings of this century.

Political Science: What legal restraints does Dr. Smith's research face?
Describe the political atmosphere at the time of Dr. Smith's experiment.
What would be different if a popular politician were to show interest
    in the results of Dr. Smith's experiment?
How can politics affect advances in science and the educational environment?

Note-Taking Tips

You've seen how a self-questioning strategy works to support your learning. Now we're going to explore another powerful learning strategy, the art of notetaking.

THE IMPORTANCE OF TAKING NOTES You may say, *I just don't think it's that important to take notes in class.* Keep in mind that your notes are your primary link to the vast amounts of information that your instructor is passing on to you. You will benefit from writing down as much information as you can.

Your class notes are also important keys to memory retrieval. Taking notes is like taking pictures on vacation. Every time you click the camera, you are capturing some information that you don't want to forget. When you look at your vacation pictures two years later, memories of your trip come flooding back. Class notes serve as important reminders of the course material you want to remember.

There are several advantages to taking class notes:

- ~ They help you pay attention to your instructor's message.
- ~ They help you organize information in ways that will improve comprehension.
- ~ They help you store the material efficiently for future retrieval and use.

Since most of the information college students receive from professors comes from lectures, good note-taking skills are critical to college success.

As you face examination time, you'll appreciate good notes that will refresh your memory. In fact, notes are so important to academic memory that if you have a class where note taking is not customary, you may still want to record your thoughts on that class sometime during the course of the day. Without notes, you have little to work with when class is over.

ENGAGING Different people with different learning styles have different ways of actively **engaging** themselves in a class. Thus, people take notes in different ways. Some students create outlines, others draw pictures, and some have a system of stars and bars. Try exploring different ways in which you can become actively engaged in your own note-taking process. Many times, your note-taking style will match your dominant intelligence.

The first duty of a lecturer: to hand you after an hour's discourse a nugget of pure truth to wrap up between the pages of your notebooks, and keep on the mantelpiece forever.

-Virginia Woolf

engage
to attract and hold fast

Know how to listen and you will profit even from those who talk badly.

-Plutarch

No matter what kind of notes you take, you will still need to *listen*, *think*, *write*, and *respond* at once to the material in order to end up with useful notes. These are not always easy tasks.

WRITING YOUR NOTES IN CLASS During class, write down as much of the lecture as possible. This is not the time to try to figure out what may or may not be important. It is also not the time to get distracted by making irrelevant doodles or going off on an interesting intellectual frolic of your own.

If you do have a relevant thought during class, quickly write it down in your notebook for later consideration. Then direct your attention back to the instructor's presentation. During the lecture, your primary task is to make sure that all information and ideas get recorded in your notes. If the instructor says, "This point is really important," be sure to put an exclamation point or some mark of emphasis next to that item.

INCREASING YOUR NOTE-TAKING SPEED Often students claim that they can't keep up with their notes during a fast-paced lecture. This is a valid concern if you are trying to write down as much of the material as possible.

You can increase your note-taking speed by developing a system of abbreviations for frequently used words. Some of the words will be unique to a subject. Others will be general words that recur often in conversation. Be sure to keep a list of terms, along with their abbreviations, on a page in your notebook. Note the examples for both types of abbreviations below:

While we are postponing, life speeds by.

-Seneca

Examples of Terms Unique to a Subject

Subject: *Psychology*

Term	Abbreviation
behavioral	B
cognitive	C
physiological	Phys
psychodynamic	Psy
humanistic	H

Examples of General Terms

Term	Abbreviation
therefore	∴
with	w/
increase	↑
decrease	↓
primary	1°
secondary	2°
that is	i.e.
for example	e.g.
et cetera	etc.
greater than	>
less than	<

If a lecture or discussion suddenly seems incomprehensible, don't panic, and don't stop writing. Continue to write everything down, but mark your notes with a question mark (?) or an asterisk (*). These symbols serve as a reminder that you will need to clarify a point later.

If you are a slow writer or a daydreamer, or if you have a fast-talking instructor, you may fall behind in your note taking. When this happens, simply skip a few lines and continue writing. At the end of the lecture, the blank lines will indicate which parts of the lecture you missed. Your next step is to get the missing notes from someone in your class or, if necessary, the instructor. Remember that you have the responsibility to obtain the lost material.

Transforming Your Class Notes

You've seen briefly how the four levels of questions can elevate your course learning to a higher level of thinking. Now let's look specifically at how you can apply these questions to your class notes.

Turning your notes into questions can revitalize your interest in class lectures and transform your notes into tools for critical thinking. Your notes can then become a way to measure your own comprehension—to find out what you really know and to find out what you don't know.

> It is in games that many men discover their paradise.
>
> -Robert Lynd

Set up your notes according to the Cornell method described below. Then, instead of putting them away until it's time to study for a test, try reading your notes over as soon as possible after each class. Finally, take a few minutes to jot down some test questions in the margin.

PAGE SETUP Draw a line down a sheet of notebook paper to make a 3-inch column on the left side of the page and a 5-inch column on the right side. Write "Questions" at the top of the narrow left-hand column. Write "Lecture Notes" at the top of the wide column on the right. Use only the right-hand pages of your notebook for notes and questions. Left-hand pages will be used later for personal comments and extra information.

> A prudent question is one half of wisdom.
>
> -Francis Bacon

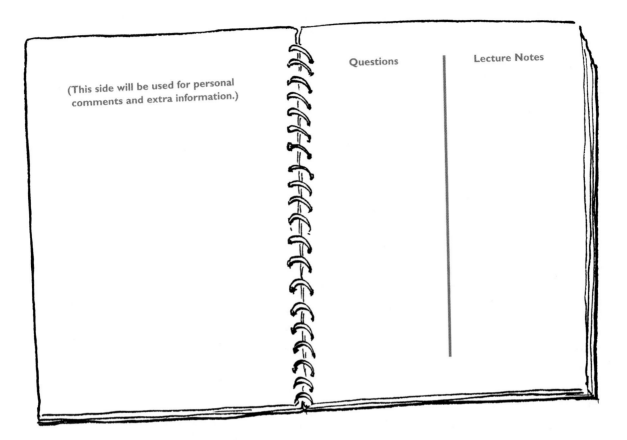

(This side will be used for personal comments and extra information.)

Questions

Lecture Notes

Once you've taken some class notes in the right-hand column, then explore some higher thought processes by creating questions on all four levels and writing them in the left-hand column. The questions should reflect the information in your notes. In other words, your notes should spark the questions you ask. Most often, the answers will be found in your notes.

When you read over your notes, first ask, *What question is this information asking?* For instance, if your instructor talked about Fort Sumter in class today, your notes might look like this by the time you added your questions.

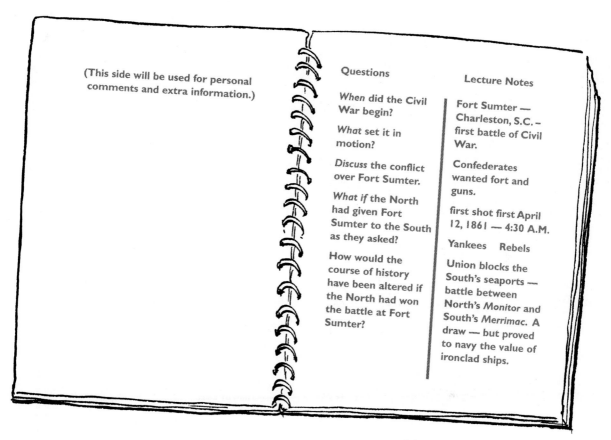

(This side will be used for personal comments and extra information.)

Questions

When did the Civil War begin?

What set it in motion?

Discuss the conflict over Fort Sumter.

What if the North had given Fort Sumter to the South as they asked?

How would the course of history have been altered if the North had won the battle at Fort Sumter?

Lecture Notes

Fort Sumter — Charleston, S.C. – first battle of Civil War.

Confederates wanted fort and guns.

first shot first April 12, 1861 — 4:30 A.M.

Yankees   Rebels

Union blocks the South's seaports — battle between North's Monitor and South's Merrimac. A draw — but proved to navy the value of ironclad ships.

Were you able to find all four levels of questions in the above example? Notice how your thinking was raised to higher levels of thought by asking a few insightful questions. These questions will probably end up on a test.

CREATING MEMORY HOOKS Once you've thoroughly explored the four levels of questions in your notes, you can create some memory hooks. Underline or highlight key words or phrases. Create acronyms or other mnemonic devices that will trigger answers to your questions. These hooks will remind you of what you've learned when you ask yourself the questions in the margin.

PERSONAL PAGE The left-hand page is for your own personal use. Use it to jot down questions for your instructor, create graphic organizers, record results of Internet searches, note new terms and examples, practice problems, draw diagrams, or do anything else that will enhance your complete understanding of the notes. When it comes time for you to really buckle down and study for a test on this material, you will have just about everything you need at your fingertips.

It is not the answer that enlightens but the question.

-Eugene Ionesco

The true art of memory is the art of attention.

-Samuel Johnson

catalyst
something that causes or
speeds up change or action

Your completed notes—transformed into a **catalyst** for critical thinking—might look something like this.

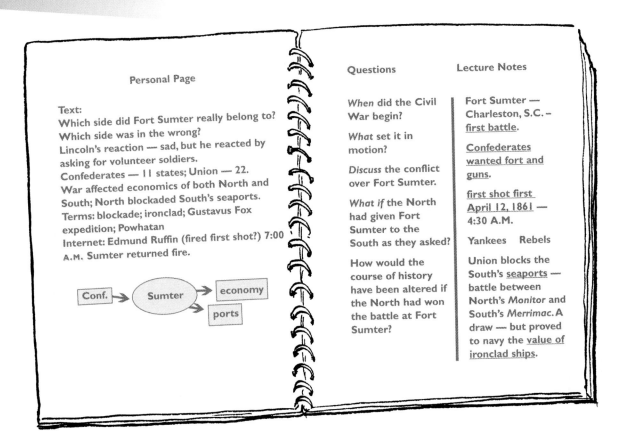

Personal Page

Text:
Which side did Fort Sumter really belong to?
Which side was in the wrong?
Lincoln's reaction — sad, but he reacted by asking for volunteer soldiers.
Confederates — 11 states; Union — 22.
War affected economics of both North and South; North blockaded South's seaports.
Terms: blockade; ironclad; Gustavus Fox expedition; Powhatan
Internet: Edmund Ruffin (fired first shot?) 7:00 A.M. Sumter returned fire.

Conf. → Sumter → economy
→ ports

Questions

When did the Civil War begin?

What set it in motion?

Discuss the conflict over Fort Sumter.

What if the North had given Fort Sumter to the South as they asked?

How would the course of history have been altered if the North had won the battle at Fort Sumter?

Lecture Notes

Fort Sumter — Charleston, S.C. – <u>first battle</u>.

<u>Confederates wanted fort and guns.</u>

<u>first shot first April 12, 1861</u> — 4:30 A.M.

Yankees   Rebels

Union blocks the South's <u>seaports</u> — battle between North's *Monitor* and South's *Merrimac*. A draw — but proved to navy the <u>value of ironclad ships</u>.

PREPARING A SUMMARY QUESTION The last step in your note-taking process is preparing a summary question. This final question sums up the entire day's material. After you recall the lecture, read over your notes, and think about the questions in the margin, then create one all-encompassing question. It will solidify your understanding and help you see how all the parts fit together to make up the whole.

Most often, summary questions are discussion questions. They may raise hypothetical *"What if…?"* questions or suggest judgments, but they depend upon a thorough understanding of the first two levels of questions. The following is a good example of a summary question for the notes on the Battle at Fort Sumter:

How would the course of history have changed if the North had handed over Fort Sumter to the South as they asked?

Another possible summary question might be:

What if the North had won the Battle of Fort Sumter and maintained its control of the fort? How might that have changed the events or the outcome of the Civil War?

Remember, summary questions should reflect the instructor's objectives for the day—not your opinion. Your response belongs on your page. As the course progresses, you can combine your daily summary questions into more complex questions that cover the material for an entire week, a month, or even a whole term.

The important thing is to be able to put the parts together to understand the whole. The example on the next page ("Seeing the Forest for the Trees") clearly illustrates how the four levels of questions will help you see the "big picture."

Understanding is a kind of ecstasy.

-Carl Sagan

Seeing the Forest for the Trees

Some students see lectures as a string of individual trees, not as part of a whole forest. As a result, they only ask individual tree questions (Level 1 question) about the material:

What is an oak tree?

What kind of tree is this?

It's better for students to see larger groupings in the form of concept questions (Level 2 question):

Compare maples and birches.

What deciduous characteristics do they share?

Excellent students see even larger groupings. They think critically about the relationships and hypothesize (Level 3 question):

What if there were more evergreens in the forest?

Would this tree be able to survive with a smaller root structure?

What type of tree would be most likely to survive a forest fire?

Sophisticated students use their knowledge of the first three levels of questions to make a judgment, form an opinion, or determine value (Level 4 question). They see the big picture and ask questions that summarize the material and the subject matter:

What is the value of preserving forest land?

Students who ask higher level questions incorporate information used in lower level questions. They build upon each level, analyzing and working with the data to create a more sophisticated understanding. The student can then see not only the trees, so to speak, but the forest as a whole.

As you make it a habit to ask yourself questions on all four levels, you will gain superior understanding and become a better student. Seeing the big picture created by your notes will elevate your thought processes and prepare you for higher education and complex decision-making situations.

Processing Your Reading Before You Read

> The man who does not read good books has no advantage over the man who cannot read them.
>
> -Mark Twain

By asking questions, you can also get an overall picture of your assigned course reading material—before you ever read it. As you look at your textbook, handouts, magazine articles, Internet sites, or any other reading assignments, you will benefit by first scanning the material for key words and phrases.

If you are able to write in your textbook, you will find it helpful to highlight or underline key words and phrases in the text. If you are unable to mark up your textbook, you can use your personal pages in your notes to write key words, comments, and questions that mirror the material. Remember to include a page reference for each note. With the reference at hand, you can always return to the text for clarification without spending a lot of time.

Sometimes just a chapter introduction or summary will give you a good enough sense of the content to give you an overall picture and stimulate questions. Take a look at the following chapter introduction. Notice what questions can be derived just from reading a few sentences.

Reading to Create Questions (Introduction)

Chapter 3: Amino Acids and Proteins

Introduction

In this chapter, we shall discuss the chemistry of the amino acids. These substances are extremely important because they are the basic building blocks of all proteins. As we shall see, amino acids can link together to form long chains. These chains can enter into a diversity of folding arrangements, thus forming different three-dimensional shapes. Recent evidence suggests that the biological function of a protein molecule is determined by its specific shape. We shall discuss protein chemistry in more detail in the latter half of this chapter, where the size, shape, and functional classes of proteins will be presented. The chemistry of the peptide bond will be discussed, along with the four different "levels" of protein structure.

Questions Generated by the Reader

What relates amino acids to proteins? Why are they in the same chapter?

Amino acids are described as the building blocks of proteins. How do they build to form a protein?

Amino acids link together to form chains. What functional groups attach at the linkage?

How does the folding arrangement that forms a 3-D shape affect the chemistry?

The shape of the protein determines the biological function. Discuss the influence of geometry and stereochemistry on function. Specifically discuss the relevance of size and shape.

What are the functional classes of protein?

What is a peptide bond?

What are the four levels of protein structure?

It is important to remember that generating questions before you actually read through all the material will save you time as well as increase your understanding. Scanning for headings or summary sentences will help you see the big picture before you take time to examine the details.

Thinking in Graphic Organizers

For some people, a single picture is worth a thousand words. A street sign that suggests a steep hill by showing a truck on an incline may elicit more caution than just words on a sign will. Because we learn well through our eyes and often remember for a long time what we have seen, graphic organizers are a particularly effective way of presenting information clearly.

You may want to add some graphic organizers to your questions in the margins of your notes. They will increase your understanding and serve as good memory hooks later.

GRAPHIC ORGANIZERS—WHAT THEY ARE Graphic organizers are pictures or diagrams that order information. They make patterns and relationships explicit. Without an organizer, you may be dealing with just a long list of terms and phrases.

A graphic organizer is useful because it requires you to recognize the underlying structure of what you are learning. For example, if you are studying the food chain, you might end up with long lists and many definitions. A graphic organizer can shorten the process and chunk all the pieces of information into a few items. Ecologists often use a simple ecological pyramid, for example, to illustrate relationships in the food chain.

2nd-level consumer
(Carnivore) **Hawk**

1st-level consumer
(Herbivore) **Rabbit**

Producer **Lettuce**

Sometimes it's easier to see actual pictures of the relationships in a sort of web.

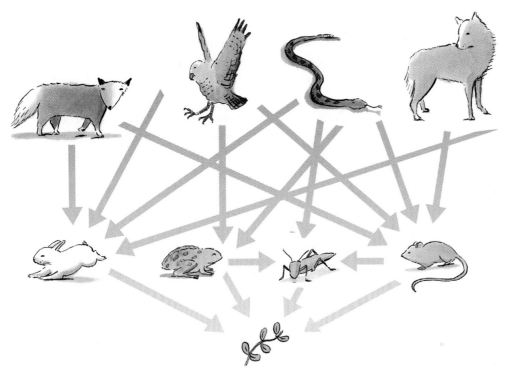

You can say a lot without using words. Just glancing at this graphic would give you a sense of which animals eat other animals in the food chain.

USING KEY WORDS WiTH GRAPHiC ORGANiZERS Some graphic organizers are called *key word diagrams* or *concept maps* because they use key words to convey meaning or define concepts. Key words carefully placed in a graphic can help you understand the relationships among numerous factors.

Look back at the example of the food chain. Some of the key words in those illustrations are obviously *producer* and *consumer*. Other key words might include *ecosystem, predator, prey,* and *energy*. Pictures combined with key words can provide powerful reminders of multifaceted or complex ideas in your notes.

CREATING YOUR OWN GRAPHIC ORGANIZERS Always approach a graphic organizer as though it has a story to tell. It's your job as the learner to figure out the story—its structure, its components, and the way all its parts fit together. In short, you are searching for meaning in the picture you make. Before you read a chapter in a book, look at the graphs, tables, pictures, diagrams, and illustrations. Try to determine what question each graphic organizer is trying to answer. Your ability to "read" graphics will serve as a sort of visual shorthand for you. For each graphic, ask yourself, *What concepts does this graphic organizer deal with? What story does it tell?* Being able to create your own graphic organizers will help you understand the graphics that are already in your textbook or supplemental readings.

As you create your own graphic organizers, be sure you first go through a sound thinking process. Know the facts and then decide what kind of relationships you want your graphic to show. Although all graphic organizers share the purpose of showing a concept in a spatial or visual manner, certain kinds of graphics might fit your subject matter better than others. Below are some examples of questions you might ask yourself before you create a graphic organizer.

- Do I want to tell a story?
- Do I want to show a sequence of events?
- Do I want to show relationships?
- Do I want to show cause and effect?
- Do I want to argue or debate pros and cons of a position?
- Do I want to show similarities and differences?

EXAMPLES OF GRAPHIC ORGANIZERS When you create a graphic, the picture should be as simple as possible and tell its story in an easy-to-remember way. Following are six examples of effective graphic organizers.

Linear Array
Uses lines to describe an event in a simple sequence

A straightforward sequence of events

~ a time line in history

1957	1958	1961	1969	1973
Sputnik I	Explorer I	First person	Apollo II	Skylab
First Russian	First U.S.	in space	First person	launched
satellite	satellite		on moon	

~ the plot sequence of a novel
~ a person's life

Progressive steps in a procedure or process

~ a math problem
~ the digestive system
~ how a bill becomes a law

Taxonomies and Hierarchies

Taxonomies show a class relationship—how different elements relate to each other. In a taxonomy, every class has its relative place, but no class is "higher" than another.

Books

Nonfiction
Histories
Criminal reports
Eyewitness accounts

Novels
Mysteries
Romances
Adventures

Life Accounts
Autobiographies
Fictionalized biographies
Letters and journals

Hierarchies also show a class relationship—how different elements relate to each other. In a hierarchy, each group has a relationship to another according to rank and preference.

Business or Corporation

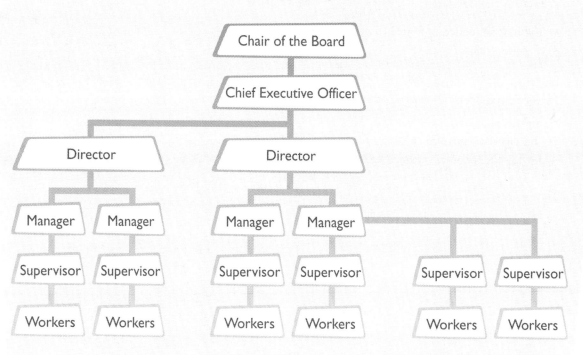

Flowchart
Shows causal relationships through a series of actions, each dependent upon the previous one

At each point, a different action or behavior could trigger a different outcome.
Flowcharts are particularly good for illustrating how one action leads to another.

IN CASE OF FIRE

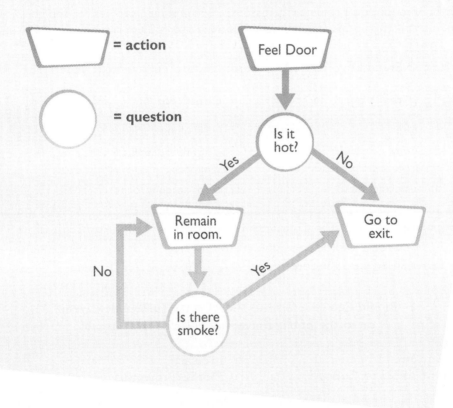

T-chart
Makes a simple representation of two sides of an issue

Pro/Con T-Chart The Pro/Con T-Chart can help when you have to make a hard decision—Should I go to a famous out-of-state college next year? Should I get a job after school? Should I go out for a varsity sport?

~ Define your question. What is it that you are debating?

~ In the Pro (positive) column, list reasons why you should say "yes" to the question. In the Con (negative) column, list reasons why you should say "no" to the question.

Should I go to a famous out-of state college next year?

Pro ("Yes")	Con ("No")
Prestigious	Make all new friends
Live away	Less family/friends support
Top program in my major	Same basic program in-state
Famous professors	Large student loans

Comparison T-Chart The Comparison T-Chart works like the Pro/Con T-Chart except you compare two different options. You will need to decide between the two alternatives, based upon the comparison.

Should I go to a famous out-of state college next year or to the public university close to my home?

Famous Out-of-State College	In-State Public University
Prestigious	Close to home
Live away	Good family/friends support
Top program in my major	Offers major in my field of interest
Famous professors	Affordable

Network
Helps you define special relationships

You may find the network graphic particularly helpful in anatomy or chemistry. You might also use it in sociology or psychology. A network lets you look at the whole picture of interactions and connections. The form the network takes and the space it covers can vary greatly, depending upon how complex your mataerial is.

Special Relationship

a species	*is part of*	a genus
a sicomac	*is a type of*	tree
critical thinking	*leads to*	understanding
the "big picture"	*is like (analogy)*	a quilt
movement	*is characteristic of*	bodily-kinesthetic intelligence
high blood sugar	*is evidence of*	diabetes

Matrix
Shows comparisons within the same category

Of all the graphic organizers, you may find the matrix the most helpful. You might compare vacation spots, schools, cars, populations, historical periods, animals, or items in any other category you can think of. The possibilities are endless. What is important is that you ask the same questions about each and that you order your answers so you can see at a glance how the groups compare on each issue.

What are the norms for the first 5 months of infant mental and motor development?

Questions	1 month	2 months	3 months	4 months	5 months
How does a baby change physically?					
How does the baby interact socially?					
What signs of acquisition language appear?					
What are the signs of cognitive development?					
What are the sensorimotor changes?					

Remember that a graphic organizer is just another collection of facts unless you understand its overall meaning—the "big picture." It's a good idea to formulate a summary question for each graphic organizer that you create.

Also remember that a summary question typically asks a *"What if…"* question. The answer sums up the main emphasis of the graphic organizer. For example, go back to the Flowchart on page 139. A good summary question for that graphic organizer would be, *What if a fire were to break out in my dorm room?*

Summary

Mastering course material by processing it at a higher level of thinking is hard work, but in the end, you will truly know what you know. You will be able to monitor your own comprehension effectively.

One of the best comprehension monitoring techniques is asking four different levels of questions about the answers you already have in your notes and reading material. Creating and answering questions that mirror the course material will result in thorough understanding, valid judgments, and well-founded opinions.

The questions are progressive—Level 1 questions (facts) must be answered before Level 2 questions (concepts), and so on. By the time you answer Level 3 questions (hypotheses), you have options from which you can choose, the foundation from which to move on to your own judgments (Level 4). Making sound, reliable judgments is what experts aim for in their particular disciplines.

Other techniques—memory hooks, summary questions, and graphic organizers—make information easier to learn and are more likely to be retrieved from your memory. These techniques take data out of the "laundry list" and put them into patterns and relationships that help you recognize their underlying structure. Graphic organizers have a story to tell, sometimes through linear arrays (time lines), taxonomies and hierarchies, flowcharts, T-charts, networks, or matrices.

Whatever technique you use to master course material, the important thing is to rise to a higher level of understanding. As you build upon information used in lower level questions and climb to analysis and judgment, you will be equipped to study smarter rather than harder. You will know what you know and you will recognize what you don't know. That is true comprehension monitoring.

Pushing your mind to higher-level questions—advanced stages of critical thinking—for all of your courses will set you on a course that will enhance your academic success in college and put you on the path to smart living for the rest of your life.

One of the greatest pieces of economic wisdom is to know what you do not know.

-John Kenneth Galbraith

What is the answer? In that case, what is the question?

-Gertrude Stein

Let's Talk

1. Describe your typical note-taking style (outlines, pictures, lists, word-for-word from the lecture, etc.). What is one of the strengths of this style? What is one of the weaknesses? After reading this chapter, how would you change your note-taking style?

2. What do you think is the most important part of notetaking? (a) listening (b) thinking (c) writing (d) responding. Explain your answer.

3. Discuss the prerequisites for answering Level 4 questions. Explain why Level 4 questions cannot stand alone. What other levels of questions cannot stand alone? Explain your answer.

4. Give at least two purposes of a summary question. Explain how summary questions can help you over the course of an entire semester.

5. One benefit of graphic organizers is that "a picture is worth a thousand words." What are at least three other benefits of using graphic organizers? Be specific.

Apply the Concepts

1. Set up a note-taking page like the example on page 128. Using your notes from a recent class lecture, transfer those notes to the page you set up. In the 3-inch margin, create questions at various levels that mirror the answers in your notes. On the left-hand page, write down any terms, unanswered questions, examples, practice problems, or graphic organizers.

2. Read each question from the list below. Then identify the LEVEL (1, 2, 3, 4) of the question being posed.

    (1)   What discipline studies the human mind?
    (2)   Compare Piaget's theory of development with that of Erikson.
    (3)   What if a person becomes fixated at a certain stage of development?
    (4)   How does Freud describe the latency period?
    (5)   Rank the personality theories of Adler, Sullivan, Horney, and Jung in terms of their applicability to Americans living in the 21st century.
    (6)   Discuss Bandura's modeling theory.
    (7)   Differentiate between gender and sex.
    (8)   Describe the "Type A" personality.
    (9)   What happens to expressive language if the part of the brain known as "Broca's area" is damaged?
    (10) Talk about the theory of development that, in your opinion, best explains human growth.

3. Take a current homework reading assignment (with or without headings). Before you actually read the material, scan through the headings and subheadings or the introductions or summary sentences. Write down key words and create questions on all four levels (facts, concepts, hypotheses, judgments). Remember, you are anticipating what the material is about by scanning and skimming before you read.

4. Think of a big decision facing you in the near future. Now create a matrix (see page 142). showing several options you have as you make your decision. (You might be comparing colleges, jobs, vacation spots, cars, etc.). After you have filled in the matrix completely and answered all the questions for each option, compare your options. Which option has the most positive responses? Which one has the most negative responses? At this point, what would your decision be?

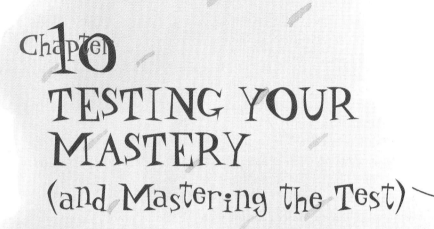

Chapter **10**

TESTING YOUR MASTERY
(and Mastering the Test)

Reviewing for a Test

Testing Yourself

Taking the Test

College Entrance Exams—a Special Case

Summary

In the previous chapter, you learned how to put your questioning strategies to work as you learn and study. You discovered the technique of generating four progressive levels of questions from your notes and your reading to test your knowledge.

Just the mere mention of the word test sometimes makes people panic. Some "test stress" comes from wondering if you really know the material that will be covered on a test, or if you've studied the right information. In this chapter, you'll discover how to relieve most of your test stress by implementing some valuable test-preparation techniques.

If you've been formulating questions in your notes and reading material, you will easily move forward to the next two steps—(1) testing your mastery of the material and (2) mastering the test. As you learn to test your own knowledge—or monitor your own comprehension—you'll be able to boost your performance on tests that come your way.

> You've got to take the initiative and play your game. In a decisive set, confidence is the difference.
>
> -Chris Evert

Reviewing for a Test

Getting ready for a test in college may take more time and organization than you are used to in high school. College tests typically cover more material and account for a substantial part of your course grade. If you're serious about succeeding in college, you'll want to be proficient at taking tests. Some college students are surprised after taking their first few tests. Although they think they know the material well, they often are not prepared for the level of course mastery that is expected of them.

You can begin your test preparation by asking yourself, *Do I really know what I think I know? Is it possible that I have just an illusion of knowing?* If you follow the suggested test-preparation techniques in this chapter, you will be able to assess whether you know the material well enough to use it on a test.

Even after college graduation, testing continues. What you know will be tested on the job, in the community, and in your personal relationships. Your part is to monitor your own comprehension so you are prepared for each test.

REVIEWING COURSE MATERIAL As a first step in preparing for a test, you will need to gather and review your notes, your reading, and any tests or quizzes that you've already taken in the course. You may want to get together with one or several other students to review and strategize.

Also try concept mapping. The purpose of a concept map is to put data into a framework that shows relationships. In a course with a lot of details, a concept map will help you organize and remember data as well as see patterns for broader ideas. A matrix is one kind of concept map. It organizes lots of information in chart form. Look at the matrix below on the terrestrial biomes of the world.

Experience is a hard teacher. She gives the test first and the lessons afterwards.

-Anonymous

MATRIX
Compare the Environmental Factors
of the Major Terrestrial Biomes* of the World

	Coniferous Forest	Deciduous Forest	Tundra	Grassland	Desert	Tropical Rain Forest	Chaparral	Savanna	Mountains
What vegetation grows there?									
What seasons are there?									
What is the topography?									
Where does it appear on the world map?									
How many inches of rain fall each year?									
What is the temperature range?									
What are the native animals?									

*__Terrestrial Biome__—A large geographical land area that contains a particular group of plants and animals and has a specific physical environment.

A matrix like this one can be used for any items that can be compared or contrasted. With categories across the top and questions down the left side (from your lecture notes, textbooks, or any other study material), the following multiple-choice test questions would be easy to predict from this matrix.

Predictable Test Questions from the Matrix

~ Coniferous forests are found in

    a. North America.   b. Asia.
    c. Europe.   *d. all of the above.

~ Burrowing rodents like prairie dogs, gophers, and ground squirrels often form large colonies in the

    a. desert.   b. savanna.
  *c. grasslands.   d. chaparral.

~ In the _____, there are three basic layers of plant growth.

    a. tundra   b. deciduous forest
  *c. tropical rain forest d. savanna

~ In a desert, only a few mammals like _____ can survive.

  *a. kangaroo rats and jerboa b. buffalo and antelope
   c. rodents and rabbits   d. giraffes and lions

*indicates correct answer

PREDICTING TEST QUESTIONS Although college instructors seldom offer review sessions, they often give exam hints during the last few classes before a test. Take very careful notes in those class sessions. Then you can start to predict what questions will be on the exam.

Teachers often ask the same kinds of questions from test to test and from semester to semester. Check with friends who have had the class before. If your history teacher always includes two essay questions on the tests, for example, then you should be prepared to answer some essay questions.

Essay questions typically call for analysis and personal interpretation of the facts. Your ability to provide a good answer to an essay question depends upon your mastery of the first three levels of questions—*fact, concept, hypothesis*—that were covered in the previous chapter. With that foundation, you can organize your thoughts and knowledge to create original evaluations and **synthesize** the data. When you really know the material, essay questions provide an opportunity for you to show the full scope of your knowledge.

If you've been formulating summary questions for your notes, reading material, and graphic organizers, then you've probably created essay questions

synthesize
to combine the parts to form the whole

already. Summary questions that cover material for an entire week, a month, or even a term, will give you clues to what will be on an essay test.

If your instructor prefers multiple-choice, true-false, or short-answer questions, then usually you will be better off predicting the first two levels of questions—*fact* and *concept*. It is important to remember, however, that even multiple-choice, true-false, and short-answer questions may require analysis or judgment.

If you don't know what kinds of questions will be on a test, ask your instructor. Most instructors are willing to explain the types of questions that will be on an exam.

Testing Yourself

Once you've reviewed all the material that will be on the test and predicted test questions, it's time to test your own mastery of the material by creating a mock exam. Since you'll want to make sure you don't have just an illusion of knowing, it's a good idea to create a practice test that includes all four levels of questions. As you create questions, you will actually be studying in depth and finding out which areas you need to study more.

TYPES OF TEST QUESTIONS Making up test questions for your mock exam is a powerful learning strategy because it is an active, rather than a passive, exercise. Instead of just thinking about the material and trying to commit it to memory, you are actually using it in a functional way. The following suggestions should help you create excellent questions for your practice test.

First, you will need to know how to write a wide variety of questions. Questions come in two basic forms—objective and analytical. The following sections describe and give examples for these two kinds of test questions.

> In preparing for battle, I have always found that plans are useless, but planning is indispensable.
>
> -Dwight D. Eisenhower

Objective Test Questions

Objective test questions require a FACT for the answer. They do not allow for your personal opinion or judgment.

TYPES OF OBJECTIVE QUESTIONS:

- **Multiple Choice**   *The tundra provides a good environment for*
  a. *gophers and coyotes.*   ***b.** *birds and insects.*
  c. *primates and snakes.*   **d.** *deer and bear.*

- **True-False**   ***T F**   *Fire is an important factor on a savanna.*

- **Short Answer**   ____(Coniferous)____ *refers to cone-bearing*
  (Simple)   *gymnosperm trees.*

BEWARE OF . . .

Qualifiers—words in a question that pinpoint whether a statement is **completely** true or **completely** false.

Qualifiers:

all, always, best, entirely, every, never, no, none, not, only, few, frequently, generally, many, most, often, ordinarily, seldom, some, usually

The following example has a qualifier. Notice how it is more difficult to choose the correct answer

   T   F   A matrix is not an effective way to organize all facts.

REMEMBER . . .

~   Objective questions are often the same questions that you created in the 3-inch margin of your notes.

~   Key words that you highlight or underline in your notes and reading material will give you clues for creating questions that cover big chunks of information and encompass the "big picture."

   *indicates correct answer

Analytical Test Questions

Analytical test questions typically come in the form of essay questions, but any type of test question may require analysis and judgment. Analytical questions require you to have a broad range of knowledge. They call for interpretation of the facts and concepts.

TYPES OF ANALYTICAL QUESTIONS:

- **Short Answer (Complex)** — *The relationship between a carrion feeder and a predator is an example of __(commensalism)__ .*

- **Essay** — *Review the environmental changes that are taking place in the tropical rain forests. Discuss what might be responsible for those changes and consider possible solutions.*

WATCH FOR ...

key words in the question. Recognizing key words is essential to completely understanding the scope of an analytical question. (See the following page for full definitions of key words in essay questions.)

REMEMBER ...

~ Essay questions usually include several aspects of your course material.

~ Essay questions often raise hypothetical considerations.

~ Your daily, weekly, and monthly summary questions often hold the key to essay questions.

Get the habit of analysis—analysis will in time enable synthesis to become your habit of mind.

-Frank Lloyd Wright

Much of your success on an essay test begins with your careful interpretation of the question being asked. Paying close attention to the meanings of key instructional words in an essay question will give you an advantage before you even start to write. Take a careful look at the meanings of the key words below. You will find many of these words on essay exams.

Essay Questions—Key Words

analyze   Separate the whole into its parts to show relationship(s), function(s), or effects.

compare   Discuss similarities between two items or issues.

contrast   Write about differences between two items or issues.

criticize   Express your judgment as to the correctness or worth of the topic being considered.

define   Explain meaning with few details.

describe   Give details (portray, explain, characterize, sketch, or tell in narrative form).

discuss   Give pros and cons with details.

enumerate   List or outline briefly, naming each of the points required.

evaluate   Show value or worth; judge the issue, using opinion, pointing out advantages and limitations.

explain   State reasons.

illustrate   Explain your answer with a figure, picture, diagram, or concrete example.

interpret   Translate, explain by example, solve, or comment on the subject, giving your judgment or reaction.

justify   Prove or show reasons for decisions; present in a convincing manner any evidence or grounds.

list   Present in an itemized series with details.

outline   Give a brief, organized description using a systematic arrangement with main points and subpoints; omit minor details.

paraphrase   Express the same ideas in your own words.

prove   Give logical reasons and well-founded evidence for the truth of something.

relate   Show connections, associations, and likenesses.

review   Examine critically; analyze and comment briefly on major points of the problem.

state   Express the main points in brief form without details.

summarize   Organize and bring main points together.

solve   Come up with a solution.

trace   Give main points from beginning to end of an event.

WRITING YOUR MOCK EXAM Now it's time to create your own mock exam. First, using some actual course material, practice writing a few test questions of your own. Make sure you feel comfortable writing each type of question before you move on. Then, devise a short test by writing several objective and analytical questions. For example, you may want to start with a short test that includes the following:

- 5 true-false questions
- 5 multiple-choice questions
- 5 simple short-answer questions
- 3 complex short-answer questions
- 2 essay questions

Be sure to make up questions that cover the material your instructor has emphasized in class. You may want to read over your class syllabus again so you can remember the course's main emphasis.

As you get more accustomed to writing good questions, you can increase the length of your mock tests. You'll soon discover that just by making a good practice exam, your comprehension and understanding of the material will increase significantly.

TAKING THE MOCK EXAM Now it's time to take your own test. It's a good idea to wait at least a day before you take your mock exam so you'll have a better chance to retain the information. Once you've taken the exam, you'll know what you still need to study. You also may want to exchange practice tests with someone else in your class. Another person's test may cover some material you've overlooked.

Don't hesitate to discuss your mock-test preparation with your instructor. College instructors have office hours for discussion and clarification of course materials. The instructor is not there to rehash the lectures or answer test questions for you, but he or she will provide some guidance. In order to get the most from your visit, come prepared in the following ways:

> Education: That which discloses to the wise and disguises from the foolish their lack of understanding.
>
> -Ambrose Bierce

- ~ If you are unclear about something, identify the problem area *before* going for help.
- ~ Bring all your course materials (notebook, textbooks, mock exam). By seeing the extent of your preparation, the instructor may notice some missing key elements.

- Write down the questions you have for the instructor. Show the instructor the methods you used (perhaps unsuccessfully) to find the answers.

- Show your instructor a copy of your mock exam to see if you've covered the important material in a comprehensive way.

Taking the Test

In addition to course knowledge, the right physical and mental preparation are critical to good test performance. Illness, fatigue, personal problems, or other factors not related to course content can affect how you perform. Here are some tips that will help you get over those mental and physical hurdles in test situations.

General Test Tips

Before the Test—Prepare Mentally and Physically

- Get a good night's sleep and eat a light, healthy meal.
- Get some exercise. Exercise relieves stress, and it helps you think more clearly.
- Take a shower.
- Get to class early—but not too early. Hurrying increases anxiety, but so does waiting.
- Pick a seat where you can see the clock and where you're away from distractions.
- Relax. Take a few deep breaths, close your eyes, think positive thoughts.

During the Test—Maintain Control

- Before you begin, glance through the entire test. Do a quick task-management plan. Pace yourself.
- Fill in all the answers you know first. This relieves anxiety and helps to trigger answers for other questions that you may not know immediately.
- Don't panic if you can't remember an answer. Take a deep breath, exhale completely, and go on to another question.
- Don't worry if other people start handing in their tests long before you are finished. They may have given up or rushed through the exam. Often, the best students finish last.

ANALYZING TEST QUESTIONS Mastering a test is essentially being in control—academically, strategically, mentally, and physically. Test success also depends on how you utilize your critical thinking abilities. By the time you take the real test, you should be confident of your ability to meet any test challenge. In every test situation, be sure to read the questions carefully and respond accordingly. A common—and needless—error stems from a student's failure to answer the question as stated. This is particularly common on essay questions. Your answer to a question that asks you to make a judgment about an event in history will not be considered correct if you merely repeat the details of what took place.

> A university professor set an examination question in which he asked what is the difference between ignorance and apathy. The professor had to give an A+ to a student who answered: I don't know and I don't care.
> -Richard Pratt
> *Pacific Computer Weekly*
> July 20, 1990

Remember: *Questions are worded carefully to evoke specific, meaningful responses.*

More than likely, many test questions you encounter in college will be Level 3 questions. In order to answer these questions effectively, you will need to draw on your critical thinking skills. In math, the instructor may ask, *What if x is greater than or less than* y? In chemistry, an instructor may ask, *What reactions would occur if the solutions were mixed?* In history, a typical question might be, *How would the course of history have been different if . . . ?* Remember, Level 3 questions require you to think through several steps before you answer the question.

~ What are the facts?
~ How do they relate to each other?
~ What would the results be if I altered these relationships in some way?

You may wonder why *"What if . . . ?"* questions are so important in college. The answer lies in the nature of higher education. In university studies, the focus is on the concepts that give meaning to the data. As a college student, you will need to know how to apply data to **theoretical** situations (*what if* contexts). You will need to do more than retain and store information. You will need to use the data you acquire to attain higher levels of thought and to understand more complex aspects of the knowledge you have.

theoretical
dealing with explanations that have not yet been proved

No matter what the level of question, every test format has its own challenges. The following Test-Taking Tips[1] will help you avoid making foolish mistakes on a test.

---

[1] Test Tips are taken from *Write for College*, Great Source Education Group, Inc.: Wilmington, MA. 1997.

Test-Taking Tips
Objective Tests

True/False Questions:

~ **Read the entire question before answering.** Sometimes the first half of a statement will be true or false, while the second half is just the opposite.

~ **Watch out for qualifiers:** Look for words like *all, every, always, never,* etc. Very often these statements will be false.

~ **Notice each word and number.** Pay special attention to names, dates, and numbers that could be incorrect.

~ **Watch for statements with more than one negative word.** *Remember:* Two negatives make a positive. (Example: It is unlikely that ice will not melt when the temperature rises above 32 degrees Fahrenheit)

Multiple-Choice Questions:

~ **Read the directions to determine whether you are looking for the correct answer or the best answer.** Also check to see if some questions can have two (or more) correct answers.

~ **Look for negative words like** *not, never, except, unless,* **etc.**

~ **Try to answer the question in your mind before looking at the choices.**

~ **Read all the choices before selecting your answer.** This is especially important on tests in which you must select the best answer, or on tests where one of your choices is a combination of two or more answers. (Example: d. Both a and b e. All of the above f. None of the above)

Matching Questions:

~ **Read through both lists quickly before you begin answering.** Note any words or phrases that are similar and pay close attention to the differences.

~ **When matching word to word, determine the part of speech of each word.** If the word is a verb, for example, match it with another verb.

~ **When matching a word to a phrase, first read the phrase, then look for the word it describes.**

~ **Cross out each answer as you find it**—unless you are told that the answer can be used more than once.

~ **Use capital letters rather than lowercase letters** since they are less likely to be misread by the person correcting the test.

Test-Taking Tips
Essay Tests

~ **Read the instructions carefully.**
How much time do you have to complete the test?
Do all the essay questions count equally?
May you use any aids such as a dictionary or a reference book?

~ **Glance over the entire test. Read the questions carefully.**
Before you can write a worthwhile answer, you must fully understand the question. Ask the instructor to clarify any word or phrase you do not understand.

~ **Pay special attention to key words in the question.** (See page 154). The key words will tell you how to present all of the information you've accumulated.

~ **Quickly jot down a task management plan.**

~ **Begin the test immediately and watch the time.** Pace yourself. Don't spend so much time on part of the test that you run out of time.

~ **Determine what level of question is being asked and then answer it appropriately.** Most often, an essay question asks a Level 3 question.

~ **Think before you write.** Come up with a thesis statement for each essay answer. Jot down all important information into a brief outline on a piece of scrap paper.

~ **Use a strong topic sentence for each paragraph.** Tie your points together with clear transitions.

~ **Use correct grammar and spelling.** Do not use abbreviations or slang.

~ **Write about the areas of the subject you are most sure of first.** Work on remaining areas as time permits.

~ **Keep your test paper neat with reasonable margins.**

~ **Revise and edit as carefully and completely as time permits.**

PLANNING TIME DURING A TEST A common difficulty that students have with tests is time. Typically, a student objects that the instructor did not allow enough time for the exam. Using task-management principles to break down the material into smaller segments will help you complete all the questions.

When tests consist primarily of objective questions (multiple choice, true-false, simple short answer), you usually can divide the test into halves or quarters and then divide up your time accordingly. In other words, if you have 40 minutes to take a test with 100 objective questions, then you should complete about 50 questions in the first 20 minutes (or 25 questions every 10 minutes).

Analytical questions in the form of an essay present more demanding time problems. Remember that you'll need to spend most of your time on the "meat" of the essay—the part that proves your point. You may want to use a task management plan like this one:

Task-Management Plan—Essay Question

20% of the time—jot down facts and main ideas
70% of the time—write the essay (introduction, body, conclusion)
10% of the time—review and improve your answer

Example: If you have 20 minutes to answer an essay question, you would divide your time like this:

Thinking and recall	4	minutes
Writing	14	minutes
Reviewing and correcting	2	minutes

AFTER THE TEST After you get a test back, be sure to review your performance.

> *Were the questions similar to the ones on your mock exam? If not, what was different?*

A low grade indicates that you were not adequately prepared.

> *Did you miss an answer because you incorrectly applied a formula or an idea, or was the question completely unfamiliar to you?*

The reason you got a question wrong is an important indicator of how you should modify your study habits for the next test. If you thought you were prepared for your calculus exam but did poorly on the test, look to see where you went wrong. Perhaps you need to do more practice problems in algebra so you can do the calculus correctly. For a history class, perhaps you need to spend more time with the textbook than you previously thought was necessary. The examination review is an extension of your learning process.

The illiterate of the 21st century will not be those who cannot read and write, but those who cannot learn, unlearn, and relearn.

-Alvin Toffler

The following checklist for "Steps to Test Mastery" summarizes the test-taking process.

Steps to Test Mastery

Prepare and Review

- ❏ Read over my notes after each class; fill in missing elements.
- ❏ Write down four levels of questions on my notes and reading material.
- ❏ Write daily, weekly, monthly summary questions.

Test Yourself

- ❏ Review notes, reading, old quizzes and tests; make concept maps or other graphic organizers.
- ❏ Avoid the "illusion of knowing" (ask myself what I know and don't know).
- ❏ Create a mock exam.
- ❏ Take the mock exam; determine what areas I need to study more.
- ❏ Make an appointment with instructor to clarify any questions.

Take the Test

- ❏ Read the questions carefully, watching out for qualifiers and key words.
- ❏ Use memory hooks.
- ❏ Practice task management during the test.

Review the Test Carefully When You Get It Back

- ❏ Understand my errors.
- ❏ Evaluate how my studying fell short.
- ❏ Analyze the test and course materials for clues to instructor's future expectations.

As you elevate your thinking and improve your study habits, you will reap the benefits—better test scores, higher overall performance, and valuable thinking strategies.

College Entrance Exams—a Special Case

One of the most intensive tests you may ever take is a college entrance exam. On several Saturday mornings each year, a total of over 1.3 million high school juniors and seniors take one of the longest and most difficult academic tests they have ever taken. Some of them take the Scholastic Assessment Test (SAT), while others take the American College Testing Assessment Test (ACT). Most colleges require test scores from one of these tests to accompany a student's application for admission. The test provides admissions officers with a "standardized" score to help them select and admit students.

Many of the test strategies that you've learned in this chapter also apply to college entrance tests. Although you won't have any material to review or recall, you can still get prepared for the test. When you take the test, your critical thinking skills will be very valuable. In addition, it's a good idea to take an in-depth course of study for the SAT that will give you the necessary practice for the verbal and the math portions of the test. Skills for the verbal portion include vocabulary skills, critical thinking skills, and critical reading skills. Necessary skills for the math portion include problem solving, reasoning, and conceptual understanding. Here are some strategies that will help you with this unique testing situation.

Test Strategies for College Entrance Exams

Take Control Before the Test

~ **Learn the rules.** College entrance exams have their own unique set of rules and strategies for attaining your personal best.

~ **Know how the test is scored.** For example, the SAT scores take into account the number of questions you answer correctly minus a fraction of the number of questions you answer incorrectly. Therefore, when you don't know an answer to a question, it is important to know how to use your critical thinking skills to make a good guess. It is also important to know when you should not guess at all.

~ **Take a pre-test.** Sample tests are available so you can get used to the test format and find out in what area you need more work.

~ **Take a course that will prepare you for the test.**

~ **Arrive for the test early and come prepared.** Know how to get to the test site. Be sure to bring all required items with you (pencils, calculator, etc.).

Be Mentally Tough During the Test

~ **Don't get discouraged.** College entrance tests contain some very difficult questions that may baffle you. It is important to keep pushing ahead and to never give up.

~ **Pace yourself.** Be aware of the clock, but don't worry about being the first one finished. Your goal should be to get your highest possible score.

~ **Remember that the questions become much harder as the test goes on.**

~ **Guessing can improve your score.** Use your critical thinking abilities to eliminate choices and guess from those left over. For example, can you name the capital of Burundi? Most students can't. Let's put the question in a multiple choice format: The capital of Burundi is (a) London (b) Calcutta (c) Moscow (d) Bujumbura (e) Mexico City. By process of elimination, can you name the capital of Burundi now?

Summary

You can test your own mastery of course material by formulating test questions that monitor your comprehension and test your knowledge and understanding. If you really know what you know, you will be able to master most tests. Creating and taking your own mock examination is one strategy in assessing your mastery of the material. A mock test also provides you with a valuable, in-depth study tool.

Formulating intelligent test questions may seem difficult at first. A thorough understanding of the different types of questions—objective and analytical—will help you create questions that test the full scope of your knowledge. As you become more skilled at writing test questions, you also will become more proficient at answering them. You will pick out the qualifiers that may change the way a question should be answered. In addition, you will be able to recognize and define key words in analytical questions, which will give you an instant advantage before you even begin writing.

Most questions for your mock exam will come directly from your notes and textbook. A question you've already created in the 3-inch margin of your notes may, in fact, appear on your actual test. As you take your mock test, you will realize what areas are causing you problems. You can then go back and study those areas or make an appointment with your instructor to clarify any lingering questions.

Although some degree of anxiety is normal, and may even be helpful during a test, your level of stress will be much lower when you have mastered your own practice exam. Your review of old tests or quizzes, as well as some concept mapping, also will prepare you for successfully mastering the test.

Before starting the test, be sure you quickly make a task management plan so you will be able to finish in the time allotted. Finally, when you get your test back, review your performance. Be sure to make review an extension of your learning process.

The strategies you have learned in this chapter and in a lifetime of taking tests will serve you well as you take college entrance exams.

Let's Talk

1. In your opinion, what kind of question—objective or analytical—tests your knowledge more effectively? Explain your answer.

2. Give an example of a true-false question. Now add a qualifier to the question, one that will change the answer.

3. How might a take-home, open-book essay test prove to be more difficult than a 20-minute essay question in class?

4. Write down at least five questions you might ask an instructor in a pre-test appointment. Make sure these questions get the most helpful information or clarification from your instructor. (Remember, you can't ask what the test questions will be.)

5. What are the main advantages of concept mapping? How does it help you master a test?

Apply the Concepts

1. Using your notes for *College Transition*, create 25 test questions. Include just objective questions (true-false, multiple-choice, simple short answer, and complex short answer). Then take your own test and evaluate your mastery of the material. (Be sure to put your answers on a separate sheet of paper.) Next, exchange tests with another classmate and take his or her test. Evaluate your performance once again. How do your two test results compare?

2. Create three good essay questions that cover the course material in *College Transition*. Be sure to use key words from "Essay Questions—Key Words" on page 154. Evaluate your questions to make sure they (1) require a mastery of facts and concepts and (2) ask for judgment or conclusion.

3. Using the essay questions prepared in question 2 above, exchange questions with a classmate. Your classmate will answer one of your essay questions, and you will answer one of your classmate's questions. When you are both finished, grade each other's essays. Since you wrote the essay question, you should be able to give many helpful comments (where reasoning was faulty, where knowledge and concepts were limited, etc.).

4. Pretend a classmate is a college instructor from whom you are seeking pre-test guidance. Role play the conference and ask your classmate to assess how prepared you were when you came to the conference, whether you asked good questions, etc.

5. Determine when your next test will be (for any of your classes). Using the "Steps to Test Mastery" on page 162, prepare for the test by following those steps and checking off each box when completed. After you have taken the test, write several paragraphs detailing what you did to accomplish test mastery. Explain how the "Steps to Test Mastery" may have improved your performance.

Part 3 Critical Thinking—
The Elements of Thought

The Process and Products of Critical Thinking

As you know by now, *College Transition* is about powerful, effective thinking. The first part of this course introduced you to the four properties of your mind—drive, action, openness, and reason. Then you discovered how to become an active, self-regulated learner, in control of your own mind, motivation, goals, and accomplishments. You learned how the four levels of questions serve as a powerful tool to help you understand and take control of your class notes and reading material.

The mind is its own self. It can make of hell a heaven or of heaven a hell.

-John Milton

Along the way, you've become well acquainted with yourself and the way you learn best. You know what it takes to acquire knowledge, retain it, and readily retrieve it with memory hooks. In addition, you know how to master course material and how to prove it to yourself and to your instructors. Overall, you're putting autonomous learning to work for you.

Now you're ready to take the next step and analyze the elements that go into critical thinking. You are ready to meet the challenge of basic *metacognition*—the act of thinking about thinking.

Thinking About Thinking

thinking
exercising the powers of
logic, judgment, and
inference

Since **thinking** is more than just having a few facts or pictures flying around in your head, your task now is to find out what really goes into your thought process. In Part Three, you'll find out what takes place in your mind when you think about an object, a person, or an idea. Then you'll discover how to use your powerful thinking process intentionally to enhance your understanding and boost your performance.

Although critical thinking is a natural ability that we utilize every day, we sometimes forget to apply it to structured assignments and conflict resolution. Critical thinking, then, must be purposely called into action. In the next few chapters, you will (1) take an intense look at how you think and reason, (2) analyze the steps that you take when you think critically, and (3) intentionally put critical thinking to work for you at will. You will be able to "turn on" your critical thinking ability in school, at home, in social situations, at your job, and in your community. At first the process may feel awkward and complicated, but once you internalize the questions you must ask, critical thinking will seem more natural.

The Need for Critical Thinking

The whole of science is
nothing more than a
refinement of everyday
thinking.

-Albert Einstein

You may wonder why you should even bother to think in such complex ways. The answer is all around you. We live in an environment in which critical thinking is not only essential but highly valued. We acclaim those who use their powerful reasoning abilities to make more powerful computers or solve the problems we have with them. We also elevate those whose critical thinking abilities give us sophisticated medical technology or amazing spacecraft that explore our solar system. Other critical thinkers devise theories that speculate on the meaning and value of life, while still others explore how we live, interact, and thrive.

On the other hand, it's probably safe to say that a very large segment of the population—perhaps even some of your own friends and relatives—do not base a lot of their thinking or their opinions on sound reasoning. Sometimes they even act on their unsubstantiated opinions with disastrous results. For example, the story is told of a woman in Chicago who tied knots in the cords of her electric appliances and her lamps in order to cut down on

Most people would sooner
die than think; in fact,
they do so.

-Bertrand Russell

the amount of electricity she used and thus save on her utility bill. Thinking—especially critical thinking—will help you recognize when your reasoning, or someone else's, is faulty or manipulative.

Some people may believe that reason-based thinking is only for philosophers. In fact, all of us benefit when each of us interacts reasonably with others. Because we can share and understand one another's reasons, we can better appreciate that which makes each of us act as we do. With shared insight, we can learn how to work together for success.

You can fool all the people all the time if the advertising budget is big enough.

-Ed Rollins
presidential campaign adviser

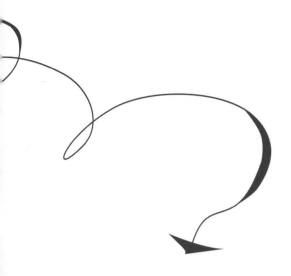

You already know how to think because you do it every day. Your mind is accustomed to analyzing situations, making assumptions, drawing conclusions, and acting upon them. Most of the time, however, you do things on "automatic pilot"—thinking, but not thinking about the process of your thinking. You normally wouldn't ask yourself, What did I think about before I sat down on that chair? You merely see a chair, have a desire to sit down, and then sit. Actually, even though you were unaware of it, your mind just went through a critical thinking process.

What presents a real challenge is first recognizing and understanding that thinking process and then checking to be sure the thinking is clear, accurate, and reasonable. What did my mind go through before I sat on the chair? Once you completely comprehend the process, you will be able to utilize it intentionally and reasonably in any situation. The key word here is intentionally. When you know how to think critically, at will, your mind becomes a powerful source for reason and sound, meaningful judgment. Your decisions are based on rational conclusions and result in effective courses of action.

The chart on the next page outlines the elements of thought necessary in a logical critical thinking process. As this chapter covers each element in detail, refer back to this chart often to keep the "big picture" in mind. The chart will be a handy reference for you later to make sure you're using the most effective thought process. The order of the elements can vary.

Simplicity is the natural result of profound thought.

-Anonymous

Elements of Thought

POINT OF VIEW
From what point of view does the analysis come?

PURPOSE
What is the purpose, goal, or end in view?

QUESTION AT ISSUE
What is the question at issue or the problem to be solved?

EVIDENCE
What is the evidence or data (known facts)?

CONCEPT
What is the central concept, or the relationship among the data?

ASSUMPTIONS
What assumptions are being made? What is being taken for granted?

CONCLUSIONS
What conclusions or inferences can you draw?
(The conclusion answers the question at issue.)

CONSEQUENCES
What are the consequences or the possible outcomes of this action?
(The consequence responds to the purpose.)

The Thought Process

Although it seems simple, all understanding of objects or actions stems from an appreciation of specific elements of thought. Knowing these basic elements and their pattern can be extremely beneficial when thinking becomes more complex and understanding presents a challenge.

AN EVERYDAY TASK Let's examine the elements of thought that go into the everyday task of sitting on a chair. (Notice how these progressive steps follow the "Elements of Thought" chart at the beginning of this chapter.) First, recognize the **object** of your thought—a chair.

Thinking Critically
(An Everyday Task) *Sitting on a Chair*

~ *From what viewpoint does the analysis come?* In this case, it is from your own viewpoint. (**point of view**)

~ *What am I asking? What am I trying to make up my mind about?* Your mind is asking, Where is a chair in this room? (**question at issue**)

~ *Why am I trying to find this out?* You'd like to sit down. (**purpose**)

~ *What are the relevant facts?* You see an object that has legs, a seat, and a back. (**data**)

~ *What concept organizes these facts?* Your experience tells you that an object that has legs, a seat, and a back is a chair. In this context, the data have a relationship. (**concept**)

~ *What assumption do I make about the data and the concept?* You were taught early that objects with a back, seat, and legs are chairs, and chairs are to sit on. (**assumption**)

~ *What can I conclude, based upon the data, concept, and assumption?* You conclude that you are, in fact, looking at a chair. (**conclusion or inference**)

~ *What do I do as a result of my conclusion?* As a result, you go over and sit on the chair. (**consequence**)

All thinking follows this same pattern. First, it is important to note that you have to have an object of your thought. The object may be a person, a thing, a formula, a problem, an idea, a story, an opinion—anything you might think about. If this sounds obvious, it's really not. Many problems in communication come from a failure to recognize the object of your thinking.

I had three chairs in my house; one for solitude, two for friendship, three for society.

-Henry David Thoreau

AN INCIDENT Next, let's analyze an incident in the same way we analyzed the everyday task of sitting down. Notice how the pattern of thinking again follows the progressive elements of thought found on the chart on page 174.

Thinking Critically
(An Incident)

Suppose someone named Fred hears a woman scream outside his window. He dashes to the window to look out, but he doesn't see the woman. He does notice two joggers looking in the direction from which the scream seemed to come. With smiles on their faces, the joggers continue to run. Fred moves away from the window and goes back to what he was doing.

Your first step is to recognize that the **object** of thought is an incident.

~ *From what viewpoint does the analysis come?* In this case, it is from Fred's viewpoint. (**point of view**)

~ *What is Fred asking? What is he trying to make up his mind about when he rushes to the window?* He's asking himself why a woman screamed, wondering if a woman is in danger and if she needs help. (**question at issue**)

~ *Why does Fred try to find this out?* He wants to know if he needs to help. (**purpose**)

~ *What are the facts in this issue?* A woman screams; joggers nearby smile while looking in the direction of the scream; they keep running. (**data**)

~ *What is the concept? What is the central idea behind the data?* Someone potentially in danger. Someone potentially guilty of harm. (**concept**) (NOTE: Exercise is NOT the central concept of this incident because exercising is not significant to the story.)

~ *What assumptions does Fred make based upon the data and the concept?* Fred assumes that the joggers are well-intentioned people, not evil people who are part of a plot to harm the woman. He assumes they would not smile if the woman were in trouble. (**assumption**)

~ *What does Fred conclude, based upon the data, concepts, and assumptions?* Fred concludes that the woman is not hurt or in danger and does not need his help. (Why she screamed is not answered, but it is clear to Fred that the reason is not something serious.) (**conclusion** or **inference**) (NOTE: The conclusion answers the question at issue.)

~ *What does Fred do as a result of his conclusion?* Fred takes no action to help the woman. He moves away from the window and goes back to what he was doing. (**consequence**) (NOTE: The consequence responds to the purpose.)

At this point, it's fair to ask, *Can thinking really be this complicated?* It is when you take it apart as the above examples have done. As soon as you become comfortable with the terms and the ideas behind them, you use critical thinking to solve the most complex problems and understand the most complicated concepts. The purpose of such thorough analysis is to provide you with a **method** to help you identify and utilize the elements of thought so you can apply them in all aspects of your life.

AN ACADEMIC EXAMPLE Let's go further with our analysis of the elements of thought by using an academic example. At this point in your education, and for several more years in college, you may find that you are using your critical thinking skills primarily in academic situations.

It is important to note that you can use the logical steps of the elements of thought in every course or subject. Each **discipline** asks its own questions and answers them in a unique way. In the study of literature, for example, the point of view most often comes from the author. You can also base your analysis on your own point of view or on the perspective of one of the characters in a literary work.

By way of an academic example, let's take a look at *The Scarlet Letter*, a novel by Nathaniel Hawthorne.

method
a procedure or process of inquiry

I do not feel obliged to believe that the same God who has endowed us with sense, reason, and intellect has intended us to forego their use.
-Galileo Galilei

discipline
a specific field of study

Critical Thinking
(An Academic Example)

In The Scarlet Letter, Nathaniel Hawthorne sheds light on the Colonial Period as he sees it from the eyes of a 19th-century Romantic. Through the results of an adulterous affair, Hawthorne reveals the ways and the motivations of American Puritans. Hester Prynne is publicly chastised for her adulterous affair with Rev. Arthur Dimmesdale by being forced to wear the red letter "A." Pearl, the child who has resulted from the affair, is lively, independent, and unpredictable. Hester and Dimmesdale seek to hide their relationship.

First, recognize that the **object** of your thought is a novel.

~ *From what viewpoint does the analysis come?* The analysis is from Nathaniel Hawthorne's viewpoint. (**point of view**)

~ *What is the question Hawthorne is trying to answer in the book?* He's asking, How did the American Puritans live? What did they believe in? Is there a more satisfactory view of life? (**question at issue**)

~ *Why did Hawthorne write about the Puritans?* He wanted to shed light on the Colonial Period as he, a 19th-century Romantic, saw it. (**purpose**)

~ *What are the facts in this issue?* Hester Prynne, a married woman, has an adulterous affair with Arthur Dimmesdale; she is publicly chastised; she raises a daughter, Pearl. Pearl is lively, independent, and unpredictable. Dimmesdale is a minister overcome by guilt. (**data**)

~ *What are the prevailing concepts?* How do the parts (and the people) relate? Sin and redemption. Adultery and Puritanism. (**concept**)

~ *What assumptions does Hawthorne make?* What is taken for granted in his point of view? Hawthorne assumes that Puritan life is harsh, unforgiving, rigid, frustrating, and self-destructive. He assumes that Romantic life, on the other hand, promises a bright future and relieves the stress of excessive guilt. Pearl is a Romantic symbol; Hester and Dimmesdale symbolize the Puritan way. (**assumption**)

~ *What does Hawthorne conclude based upon the data, concepts, and assumptions?* Hawthorne concludes that the Puritan ethic was confining and, perhaps, destructive. He values more openness and the expression of a free spirit. (**conclusion or inference**)
(NOTE: The conclusion answers the question at issue.)

~ *How does Hawthorne respond to his conclusion?* He has Pearl, the symbol of freedom from Puritan restraints, live happily ever after. In this way he shows he prefers the Romantic view of life. (**consequence**)
(NOTE: The consequence responds to the purpose.)

Think about what would happen to this critical thinking about *The Scarlet Letter* if you were to change the answer to the first question by altering the point of view. How would any of the elements be different if the analysis took place from *your* point of view instead of Hawthorne's?

If you were careful to answer the questions for each element of thought, you might end up with a different conclusion. Though different from Hawthorne's, your conclusion would still be valid if you used all the elements of thought in a reasonable way.

Teachers often return assignments with comments that point directly to the absence of one or more of these elements of thought. If you are careful to cover all the elements in your academic work, you will avoid these lapses of reason and keep in touch with what is central to sound thinking.

Following are comments that teachers frequently write on papers to show where a student's reasoning is misguided. These comments call your attention to the basic tenets of good critical thinking. Notice how each one directly relates to a missing element of thought.

Teacher Comments
That Point to the Elements of Thought

TEACHER'S COMMENT	MISSING ELEMENT OF THOUGHT
Which side are you arguing?	The **point of view** is not evident.
Where are you going with this?	The **purpose** is unclear to the reader.
What question are you trying to answer?	The **question at issue** is not explicit.
You need to back this up.	The paper is lacking in **data** (evidence).
How do these ideas relate to each other?	The central **concept** is not identifiable.
Is this true? How do you know?	The **assumptions** are either not clear, not well supported, or don't work.
You're making a leap here. Does this follow?	The **conclusion** or **inference** doesn't make sense. The concepts, data, and assumptions don't support the conclusion.
Have you considered _____ in your argument?	The **consequence** is invalid because critical facts have not been considered.

Analyzing the Elements of Thought

Now that you have an overall view of what critical thinking is and how it works as a progressive thought process, it's time to look at each element individually.

Point of View

Question: *From what point of view does the analysis come?*

Fact: To get an accurate understanding of anything, you must recognize the point of view of the object to be analyzed, as well as the point of view of the one doing the analysis. If you are asked to analyze something from another person's point of view, try to put yourself in his or her shoes.

Remember:

~ Point of view is simply a **standpoint**—a position from which the object or idea is viewed and according to which it is compared and judged.

~ Point of view is not a **stand**—it is not an opinion.

~ Point of view influences the answers to all the other questions in the elements of thought.

> Think not that thy word and thine alone must be right.
>
> -Sophocles

standpoint
a position from which objects or principles are viewed and according to which they are compared and judged

stand
a strongly held position on a debatable issue; an opinion

Purpose

Question: *What is the purpose, goal, or end in view?*

Fact: Whenever you reason, you expect to achieve some purpose or fulfill some need. The purpose often provides the basis and the explanation for the question at issue or the problem to be solved.

Remember:

~ If the purpose is unrealistic, confusing, or contradictory, your reasoning will be defective.

~ In the end, the purpose is satisfied in the last element of thought (*consequence*).

Question at Issue

Question: *What is the question at issue or the problem to be solved?*

Fact: Reasoning or critical thinking always involves at least one question or problem to be figured out.

Remember:

~ If the question is unclear, your reasoning will be misguided.

~ The question at issue must relate to the purpose, goal, or end in view.

~ If the question is unclear or does not relate to the purpose, your "answer" (conclusion or inference) will not meet the purpose or goal.

Evidence

Question: *What is the evidence or data (known facts)?*

Fact: We need some material to fuel our reasoning.

Remember:

~ Always remain clear about the difference between data and opinions.

~ Choose only data relevant to your question or problem.

Concept

Question: *What is the central concept, or the relationship, among the data?*

Fact: All reasoning deals with certain concepts (ideas, theories, relationships, principles, rules). The central concept is influenced by the **context** in which the data exist.

context
the conditions or circumstances that surround an event or situation

Remember:

~ Think of the object or idea under analysis as a Web page. What key word(s) would result in this Web page coming up at the top of a search? That term is your central concept.

~ If your concept is wrong or unclear, your conclusion or inference will be incorrect.

Assumptions

Discovery consists in seeing what everyone else has seen and thinking what no one else has thought.

-Albert Szent-Gyorgi
1937 Nobel Prize in Physiology and Medicine

Question: *What assumptions are being made? What is being taken for granted?*

Fact: All reasoning must begin somewhere and make some assumptions or take some things for granted. For example, most people don't talk about why they know that a chair is really a chair. They just assume that a chair is really a chair from their past experience.

Remember:

~ If an assumption is faulty, the reasoning process that follows will also be faulty.

~ Assumptions vary from person to person due to differences in backgrounds.

Conclusion

inference
something concluded by reasoning from known facts or evidence

Question: *What conclusion or* **inference** *can you draw?*

Fact: All reasoning proceeds in a series of steps: "If this is so, then this is also so (or probably so)." Eventually, the reasoning process results in a final conclusion, inference, or judgment.

Remember:

~ A conclusion answers the question at issue.

~ Conclusions and inferences are not determined just by data and concepts. They are also determined by the assumptions you bring to the data and the concepts.

Consequences

Question: *What are the consequences or the possible outcomes of this action?*

Fact: The consequence of thinking is decision or action.

Remember:

~ The consequence satisfies the purpose inherent in the problem.

~ Reaching a particular conclusion calls for a corresponding reaction or behavior.

The elements of thought have been put in a particular order for ease of understanding. It is significant to emphasize, however, that there is no required order for answering these questions. Depending on the issue being analyzed, some questions will naturally be answered before others. Nonetheless, it is important that you consider all questions. Once the questions are answered to your satisfaction, you can complete your analysis with two final steps: (1) recognize other options or variations that might alter your conclusion, and (2) make any necessary changes to your final judgment.

Exercises in Critical Thinking

EXERCISES IN CONCEPT *Point of view, purpose, question at issue,* and *evidence (data)* are usually somewhat straightforward, easy-to-answer questions when you make your way through the elements of thought. Thus we will start with an exercise for the element of *concept*.

> People demand freedom of speech to make up for the freedom of thought which they avoid.
>
> -Kierkegaard

For each of the following exercises, find the unifying *concept* by examining the relationship among the facts. Since concepts deal with relationships among data, the most direct way to get to the concept is to ask, *How are these things related?* You should be able to write the concept in a few words.

1. **Data**   Judaism, Islam, Christianity, Buddhism

   Concept   _____

2. **Data**   Hershey Kisses, Twizzlers, M&Ms, Starburst

   Concept   _____

3. **Data**   dress code, compulsory attendance, honor code, grading system

   Concept   _____

4. **Data**   Do not kill; do not steal; honor your mother and father; do not commit adultery

   Concept   _____

5. **Data**   democracy, oligarchy, dictatorship, autocracy

   Concept   _____

(Suggested answers to the above exercises can be found at the end of the chapter.)

EXERCISES IN ASSUMPTION Each of the following exercises analyzes a situation using all the elements of thought. All information is provided except the assumption. Examine each scenario and determine the central assumption for each one.

1. **Point of View**   a concerned parent

   Question at Issue Should I spank my child?

   Purpose   to restore order

   Data   child frequently misbehaves, disrupts order

   Concept(s)   child rearing, proper behavior

   Assumption   _____

   Conclusion   Children should be spanked.

   Consequence   child is spanked

2. **Point of View**   nonsmoking taxpayer

   Question at Issue Should smokers get public health insurance?

   Purpose   to assure fairness

   Data   smoking-related illnesses, increasing cost of insurance premiums

   Concept(s)   public health policy

   Assumption   _____

   Conclusion   Smokers should not get public health insurance.

   Consequence   Support legislation to exclude smokers from receiving public health insurance.

(Suggested answers to the above exercises can be found at the end of the chapter.)

EXERCISES IN ALL THE ELEMENTS Now that you've had some practice with individual elements, try analyzing a complete critical thinking situation. In the first exercise, you will need to do an analysis from your point of view as though you were the babysitter. Keep in mind that different babysitters might have different ways of looking at this problem. You should be concerned only with your own viewpoint.

Exercise #1 — General Topic
"The Babysitter"

Two little children are playing together. One child wants to play "pirates"; the other child wants to play "neighbors." They get into an argument about which one they will play. You are in charge of watching the children. Do an elements-of-thought analysis of the situation to determine what to do.

Point of View:	You (the babysitter)
Purpose:	
Question at Issue:	
Evidence (Data):	
Concepts:	
Assumptions:	
Conclusion:	
Consequence:	

Following is a completed version of this analysis. As you compare your version to this one, keep in mind that your answers may be different and yet still be correct. What you do need to watch for, however, are any areas in which you used faulty or unsupported reasoning.

Exercise #1 — General Topic
Complete Analysis
"The Babysitter"

Two little children are playing together. One child wants to play "pirates"; the other child wants to play "neighbors." They get into an argument about which one they will play. You are in charge of watching the children. Do an elements-of-thought analysis of the situation to determine what to do.

Point of View: the babysitter

Purpose: *to restore order; to end an argument*

Question at Issue: *How can I successfully resolve this conflict?*

Evidence (Data):   *Two children are playing; one child wants to play "pirates"; the other wants to play "neighbors." They are fighting over what they will play.*

Concepts: *conflict and its resolution*

Assumptions: *(a) punishment is a viable approach to conflict resolution.*

(b) fairness is the most important component of conflict resolution.

(c) children should learn to resolve conflicts through interaction.

Conclusion: *These conclusions correspond to the above assumptions:*

(a) punish the children.

(b) give equal time to both activities.

(c) leave the children alone to work out their disagreement and discover their own alternative.

Consequence: *These actions correspond to the above assumptions and conclusions:*

(a) send the children to their rooms; forbid them to play together.

(b) ask the children to play a half hour of "pirates" and a half hour of "neighbors."

(c) unknown—depends on the children's resolution. Example: They might agree to play "pirate neighbors" (a new game).

Now that you've practiced the elements of thought in a complete critical thinking situation with a general topic, try the academic example below.

Exercise #2 — Academic Topic
"The Poem"

You have been given the following poem to interpret for your English class.

The Unexplorer

There was a road ran past my house

Too lovely to explore.

I asked my mother once—she said

That if you followed where it led

It brought you to the milkman's door.

(That's why I have not traveled more.)

—Edna St. Vincent Millay

> In science one tries to tell people, in such a way as to be understood by everyone, something that no one ever knew before. But in poetry, it's the exact opposite.
>
> -Paul Dirac

Point of View: The author (Edna St. Vincent Millay)

Purpose: _____

Question at Issue: _____

Evidence (Data):   _____

Concepts: _____

Assumptions: _____

Conclusion: _____

Consequence: _____

Now compare your answers to the following sample. Answers may vary, but be sure you can defend your answers based on relevant data, clear reasons, and well-founded conclusions.

Exercise #2 — Academic Topic
Complete Analysis
"The Poem"

You have been given the following poem to interpret for your English class.

The Unexplorer

There was a road ran past my house
Too lovely to explore.
I asked my mother once—she said
That if you followed where it led
It brought you to the milkman's door.
(That's why I have not traveled more.)

—Edna St. Vincent Millay

Point of View: The author (Edna St. Vincent Millay)

Purpose: *Why did the author write this poem?*

Question at Issue: *What emotion does that author's experience evoke?*

Evidence (Data): *lovely road going by house; questions where it goes; mother's answer is "milkman's door"; author will not travel down the road*

Concepts: *interest in travel; title suggests explorer as well*

Assumptions: *milkman is not exciting; milkman's home is an everyday, humdrum destination; only romantic, adventurous travel is worthwhile*

disillusioned
disappointed or dissatisfied

Conclusion: *author is **disillusioned** about the road; decides not to travel more [answers question at issue]*

Consequence: *author wrote the poem to express model for disillusionment [answers purpose]*

Once you have a handle on the author's purpose for writing the poem, you are in a position to think about the extent to which the author is successful. You will then want to ask the questions from your own point of view to determine your appreciation (or lack of appreciation) of the poem.

Summary

- -

Critical thinking is a natural reaction to many things that we face in everyday living. It can also be a learned method of thinking that we can utilize at will. Critical thinking assesses the scope and range of an issue through conscious reasoning.

In the academic realm, we think differently for each discipline, approaching each subject according to its uniqueness. The elements of thought, however, are common to all areas of study, whether English, science, history, mathematics, or some other subject.

The way you think will affect your occupational future. No longer can a person learn only simple tasks and expect to be competitive in a changing job climate. The responsibilities of a mechanical engineer twenty or thirty years from now will be extremely different from those of today. The only way to keep up in this fast-changing world is to solidify those critical thinking skills that readily adapt to change.

If you can take apart a difficult problem today and reach a good solution, you will surely be able to do it tomorrow, and the next day, and the day after that. In time, the problems will change, but the skills you use to solve those problems—your ability to think critically—will remain the same. Keep in mind that critical thinking is **transferable thinking**—thinking that can be used in many different contexts and situations.

IMPACTING THE WORLD By now, you may be wondering why thinking is so important. You may clearly understand how good reasoning relates to your homework assignments and even how it will help you out in your personal life and your future career. But the importance of logical analysis reaches much further than these areas of your life. Your ability to think critically could affect the way you personally impact the world.

In a world where people have the ability to destroy themselves and the planet, even one person's critical thinking skills could make a difference. In an environment where diseases, new strains of viruses, and tougher mutated cells demand more solutions, just one critical thinker could make a difference.

The fast track of technology will compel more and more people to live and work with higher levels of problem-solving aptitudes than ever before. As our goals get more complex and solutions more complicated, our thinking

Almost everyone has had occasion to look back upon his school days and wonder what has become of the knowledge he was supposed to have amassed during his years of schooling, and why it is that the technical skills he acquired have to be learned over again in changed form in order to stand him in good stead... But [knowledge] was segregated when it was acquired and hence is so disconnected from the rest of experience that it is not available under the actual conditions of life.

-John Dewey
Experience and Education, 1938

It has become appallingly obvious that our technology has exceeded our humanity.

-Albert Einstein

capabilities must increase at the same rate. However, these powerful abilities of the mind must help to improve rather than destroy our world.

Critical thinking also provides protection for a democratic government. People who think with reason make sound political decisions and run governments rationally. Democracy, in theory as well as in practice, depends on an educated, critically-thinking public. Consider some of the great changes in the history of the United States that were products of effective critical thinking.

The Emancipation Proclamation of 1863, which declared all enslaved people free, was the result of people analyzing the values of the Constitution and concluding that the holding of slaves contradicted those values. Women's right to vote came after intense analysis and sorting of the issues. The same is true for the desegregation of schools. Each change required the leaders of our country, as well as the voting public, to think critically.

You now have an arsenal of insights to help you think with reason. If you know how to use the elements of thought, you will be more likely to see relationships among a problem's sophisticated data. Your assumptions will be sound, and your conclusions will reflect a full awareness of the issues and their ultimate impacts upon the world.

There is no question that someday you will be asked to use your powerful reasoning abilities to make your mark on the world. Whatever your "world" may be, it will at some point depend upon you to think critically and reasonably. Your world requires you to be ready.

Answers to Exercises in Concept on page 183: Answers may vary slightly. Most likely, the concepts will be as follows: (1) world religions (2) candies (3) school regulations (4) biblical commandments (5) governments.

Answers to Exercises in Assumption on page 184: Assumptions will vary. Likely answers will be: (1) Spanking is an appropriate method of discipline. (2) Smoking is a matter of choice; non-smokers should not have to be economically responsible for smokers' poor choices.

Let's Talk

1. What is the difference between thinking on "automatic pilot" and thinking intentionally?

2. Explain in detail how changing the *point of view* alters the entire critical thinking process. Give examples.

3. From what sources do our assumptions come? What are the results of faulty assumptions? Be specific.

Apply the Concepts

1. Using all the elements of thought, analyze in writing an everyday task (brushing your teeth, eating, walking to your next class, etc.).

2. For this assignment, use the information provided for *The Scarlet Letter* on page 178. Answer the questions for each element of thought from your *own* point of view. How are your answers different from Hawthorne's? How are they the same?

3. Choose an academic assignment you currently have in one of your classes. It can be an analysis (assignments in literature, history, economics, sociology, or the like work well) or a problem-solution (assignments in courses related to math or science work well). Do a thorough critical thinking analysis in writing. Be sure you incorporate all the elements of thought.

Chapter 12

ARGUMENTATION
The Art of Persuasion

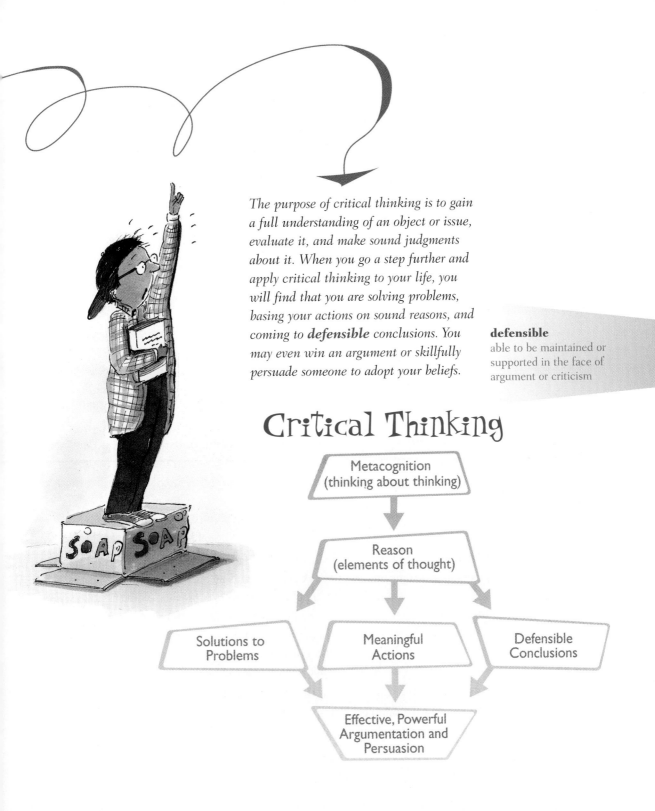

The purpose of critical thinking is to gain a full understanding of an object or issue, evaluate it, and make sound judgments about it. When you go a step further and apply critical thinking to your life, you will find that you are solving problems, basing your actions on sound reasons, and coming to **defensible** conclusions. You may even win an argument or skillfully persuade someone to adopt your beliefs.

defensible
able to be maintained or supported in the face of argument or criticism

Critical Thinking

Metacognition
(thinking about thinking)

↓

Reason
(elements of thought)

↓

Solutions to Problems

Meaningful Actions

Defensible Conclusions

↓

Effective, Powerful Argumentation and Persuasion

A Critical Analysis of Argument

- -

arguing
struggling in opposition;
contending

argumentation
the act of forming reasons
and of drawing conclusions
and applying them to an
issue being discussed

persuade
to cause a person to believe
something or do something
by appealing to reason and
understanding

It's important to note that there is a difference between everyday **arguing** and **argumentation**. Much of the arguing we do is simply voicing an opinion (*Chocolate is the best kind of ice cream—no, it's vanilla!*). You may be arguing your point of view merely from emotional conviction, not from rational evidence.

Arguing has no purposeful end. If you truly want to **persuade** someone to adopt your point of view (if you want to "win the argument"), you must show, through reasoning, that your evidence supports your claim.

The ability to persuade through argumentation will benefit you in every area of your life, from personal relationships to career ambitions. In one study, a group of economists considered a number of people—lawyers, public relations specialists, sales representatives, counselors, administrators, and others. All of their jobs depended, for the most part, upon their ability to persuade people to adopt their points of view. The economists concluded that persuasion accounts for 26 percent of the U.S. gross domestic product![1]

Persuasion—through argumentation or debate—occurs in two forms: (1) in a speaking situation where there are two or more differing opinions; or (2) in a written situation in which someone defends an idea or an issue. As you take a position in either circumstance, you must supply more than mere facts to support your point. Remember that facts are always open to different interpretations. Every **good argument** or debate has three main elements: (1) *claim*, (2) *evidence*, and (3) *rationale*.

good argument
a position that provides
justification for accepting
its conclusion

CLAIM First, an argument must make a claim or advance a conclusion that a person is attempting to prove. A claim begins as a statement or a hypothesis and ends up as a defensible conclusion when it is proved. Note the following claim: *Chocolate ice cream is the most popular flavor.* You may not agree with this claim at all. You might believe that vanilla ice cream is the most popular flavor. A claim brings with it a challenge to prove that the statement is true. Proving that a claim is true takes supporting evidence.

EVIDENCE Types of evidence that support a claim include relevant facts, representative samples, examples, and conclusions of experts, to name only a few. All evidence, however, must somehow be verifiable or provable.

[1] Bennett, Amanda, "Economics + Meeting = A Zillion Causes and Effects," *Wall Street Journal*, January 10, 1995, B1.

The following relevant facts might be used as evidence for the ice cream claim above: *Whenever I go down to the ice cream parlor, 8 out of 10 people are eating chocolate ice cream.* This may be enough evidence for some people, but further reasoning is necessary. You may have to link your claim and your evidence together with a logical **rationale**—the reasoning you construct to support your opinion with the evidence you have.

RATIONALE Clearly stated, a rationale is reasoned persuasion. It supports a convincing conclusion on the basis of sound evidence. You will not be very persuasive unless your rationale—your reasoning—is clear and logical. Consider this rationale for the ice cream example:

Though I have not visited every ice cream parlor in the world, nor taken a poll of all ice cream eaters, it still seems safe to say that the people at my local ice cream parlor represent a good sample of ice cream eaters. Therefore, what appears to be the case at my local ice cream parlor may very well be the case at all ice cream parlors.

This rationale makes your evidence much more convincing. It takes your evidence—your local ice cream parlor—and connects it to your claim through persuasive reasoning. Notice the key words and phrases used in this reasoning process:

Though... [state the weakness of your evidence]*...it still seems safe to say...* [state your known evidence]*...represent a good sample...* [show the connection of your evidence to your claim]*...Therefore...* [state your conclusion]*....*

If you look back at the process of critical thinking in Chapter 11, you will see how the elements of thought are comparable to the elements of argumentation.

~ The **claim** in an argument can be compared to a ***conclusion*** in critical thinking. A claim takes a position on a certain point and answers a central question. A conclusion answers the *question at issue*.

~ The ***evidence*** in an argument and the **evidence** in critical thinking are the same—data (known, verifiable facts).

~ The **rationale** of an argument reflects the **assumption** in critical thinking. Rationales link together the claim and the evidence. Assumptions connect the conclusion to the data.

rationale
the reasoning behind an argument that uses fundamental evidence to support an opinion or belief

. . . unless we can find other and better principles on the instant, I am certain not to agree with you; no, not even if the power of the multitude could inflict many more imprisonments, confiscations, deaths, frightening us like children with hobgoblin terrors.

-Socrates
(from *The Crito*)

Rational Rationales

It is important for you to pay close attention to rationales because they, like assumptions, are the most controversial part of an argument. Since rationales are the reasoning behind your evidence, be sure your rationales are rational. If your reasoning is faulty, then your argument will not be convincing.

Sometimes assumptions are made unconsciously or without really thinking about them. Keep in mind the example of the chair in Chapter 11. Originally, you didn't think consciously about your assumption that a chair is actually a chair. Neither would you have to convince many people that a chair is a chair. Rationales, on the other hand, are used consciously to prove a questionable assumption to be true.

FOUR BASIC CATEGORIES There are many types of rationales. For our purpose, we will look at four basic categories. Keep in mind that most rationales, if constructed poorly, become potential **fallacies**, or errors in reasoning. Pay close attention to the fallacy definitions and guidelines for avoiding them in order to avoid many common errors of argumentation.

fallacy
an error in reasoning;
logically unsound argument

Inductive Generalizations

EXPLANATION

When you make an inductive generalization, you are saying that what is true of some is true of more (or maybe all). Your reasoning moves from *particular facts* to a *general conclusion*.

A generalization always has a class (people or things) for a subject. When you make a generalization, you are saying that if *part* of a class has a certain property, then the class as a *whole* probably has that property.

Think of the general conclusions you hear in conversations: Politicians are corrupt; physics courses are hard; Marines are tough; cafeteria food is awful. Where do these conclusions come from? They come from observing particular politicians, physics courses, Marines, and cafeteria food.

EXAMPLES

Example #1:

Fact 1:   *Chocolate ice cream is my favorite.*

Fact 2:   *The students in my psychology class prefer chocolate ice cream 2 to 1.*

Fact 3:   *According to a nationwide survey, more people eat chocolate ice cream than any other flavor.*

Conclusion: *Chocolate ice cream is most people's favorite flavor.*

Example #2:

Fact 1:   *My art course last term was easy.*

Fact 2:   *My sister's art course last year was easy.*

Fact 3:   *My friend's present art course is easy.*

Conclusion: *Art courses are easy.*

COMMON FALLACY

You can make errors in inductive generalizations by making *hasty generalizations*—jumping to conclusions on the basis of insufficient evidence.

GUIDELINES

To prevent errors in reasoning:

~ Avoid hasty generalizations.

~ Make sure you have a large and relevant enough sampling of facts to justify your conclusion.

~ Make sure your facts are fair, unbiased, and representative or typical.

In example #2 above, you might well have asked yourself, *Are three art courses enough to conclude that all art courses are easy?* You also may have wanted to ask, *Are these three art courses typical of most art courses?*

Remember: No inductive generalization is reliable unless it is based on a representative sample.

Deductive Generalizations

EXPLANATION

A deductive generalization is the opposite of an inductive generalization. It moves from a general principle to a specific conclusion. You are saying that what is generally true of most is therefore true of some or of one.

A deductive generalization uses a broad, general principle to persuade people that the same principle applies to a minor premise. When your general principle and minor premise are sound, people will be much more likely to accept your conclusion.

EXAMPLES

Example #1:

One of the clearest examples of this rationale comes from American history—from Susan B. Anthony's famous speech "Is It a Crime for U.S. Citizens to Vote?" In 1872 and 1873, at a time when women were barred from voting, Anthony's speech argued along the following lines:

General Principle: *The United States Constitution guarantees all U.S. citizens the right to vote.*

Minor Premise: *Women are U.S. citizens.*

Specific Conclusion: *Therefore, the United States Constitution guarantees women the right to vote.*

Example #2:

General Principle: *Most people in the United States speak English.*

Minor Premise: *I met some Americans when I was in Spain.*

Specific Conclusion: *Therefore, those Americans probably speak English.*

COMMON FALLACY

A common weakness of a deductive generalization is a failure to support your general principle or minor premise with sound data. You will need to establish strong evidence for your general principle before moving on to your minor premise, which also must be adequately supported.

GUIDELINES

To prevent errors in reasoning:

~ Establish strong evidence for your general principle before moving on to your minor premise.

~ Establish strong evidence for your minor premise.

~ Now you can feel confident going on to your conclusion. Your "audience" will take you seriously and your argument will be persuasive.

Causal Reasoning

EXPLANATION

Causal reasoning is your attempt to support a claim by proving cause and effect—that one thing causes another. (If Y follows X, then X was the cause of Y.) The relationship between cause and effect is not always as easy as it seems.

To use causal reasoning, you need at least two circumstances, one following the other: One specific event (X) that is the cause of some other specific event (Y). You assume that if Y followed X, then X was the cause of Y. Sometimes this reasoning is valid, but be careful not to oversimplify cause and effect.

EXAMPLES

Examples of Causal Reasoning:

Because the road was covered with ice, my car slid off the road.

If the road hadn't been ice-covered, my car would not have slid off the road.

Examples of Causal Claims (which have a foundation of causal reasoning):

Smoking causes birth defects.

The new antibiotic prevents infection.

Vitamin C does not cure colds.

COMMON FALLACY

A common error of causal reasoning is **false cause**—mistakenly assuming that because one event follows another, the first event must be the cause of the second. This fallacy is often known by its Latin name, *post hoc, ergo propter hoc*, meaning "after this, therefore because of this."

Here are three good examples of false cause:

Gun control does not decrease violent crime. Just look at Utah. They passed a strict gun-control law, and what was the result? Crime increased.

Every time I see a fire, I see firemen around. Firemen must cause fires.

According to a study by the American Medical Association, men with bald spots have three times the risk of heart attack as men with a full head of hair. It looks as if baldness is a cause of heart attacks.

GUIDELINES

To prevent errors in reasoning:

~ Remember that just because one event happens after another, the first event is not necessarily the cause of the second.

~ Don't assume that events have only one cause. In fact, most events have several causes.

~ Try not to attribute complex events to simple causes. For example, the cold war began just a few months after dropping the atomic bomb on Hiroshima and Nagasaki. It would be wrong, however, to assume from that information that the cold war was caused by the bombing.

Analogic Reasoning

EXPLANATION

Analogic reasoning compares two similar situations and assumes that what is true for the first situation is also true for the second. It may also imply that if one or more items has a certain property, then a similar item must also have that property.

You must pay attention to the structure, pattern, format, and details of the situations being compared. If the situations being compared are essentially alike, the analogy is valid. If they are not essentially alike, the analogy is invalid.

EXAMPLES

Example #1:

A household that does not balance its budget will end up in financial trouble. Surely, if the federal government does not balance its budget, it will also be in financial trouble.

Example #2:

Oregon has a bottle-return law like the one proposed here in our state. The Oregon law has cleaned up the highways and improved the landfill situation. It will do the same here.

Example #3:

Many students who have studied critical thinking have been successful in their chosen careers. Mary should study critical thinking so she also will be successful.

Example #4:

Four of my friends own the same kind of car as I do. All of their cars are developing transmission problems. My car will probably have transmission problems, too.

COMMON FALLACIES

A common fallacy in analogical reasoning is making an ***invalid analogy***— comparing two situations that are not essentially alike. For instance, suppose you made the following claim: *Senator Goodsmith has been an excellent senator. Therefore, he will make an excellent President of the United States.* At first, these two situations seem comparable since they both involve federal politics. The differences, however, may outweigh the similarities. How much alike are the positions of senator and president? Is it possible for someone to be an excellent senator and not be an excellent president?

Another example of invalid analogy:

Brand X gives you the cleanest wash (cleanest compared to what?)

GUIDELINES

To prevent errors in reasoning:

~ Use truly parallel situations.
~ Use valid analogies.
~ Remember that what is true for one situation must be true for the other.

Common Fallacies

Your argumentation skills will strengthen as you use conscious rationales more and more. If you are the one doing the persuading, you will do well to leave fallacies out of your arguments. You won't lose many "arguments" if you avoid the fallacies that often creep into the reasoning process. If you are the listener, you will need to be alert and recognize when someone else is attempting to convince you with a fallacy.

There are many fallacies common to faulty argumentation—too many to mention here. You've already learned about *hasty generalization* (page 197), *false cause* (page 199), and *invalid analogy* (page 200). In addition, you will want to be aware of several other common fallacies that often sneak into your own claims and those made by others.

AD HOMINEM Ad hominem, which is Latin for "against the man," is a fallacy in reasoning that emphasizes the person rather than the real issue. For example:

He must be an awful person. He lives right next door to a well-known slumlord.

She must be a wonderful person. She belongs to a lot of fine women's clubs.

The Nazis thought the theory of relativity was wrong because it was developed by a Jew, Albert Einstein.

The senator has a number of interesting economic proposals, but let's not forget that she comes from a very wealthy family.

It is worth noting, however, that a person's character or integrity may, at times, be a legitimate issue—a police officer who violates the law, a company president who embezzles money, a scientist who falsifies research data. Raising questions about the person in such cases would not make you guilty of using an ad *hominem* fallacy.

> "You should say what you mean," the March Hare went on.
>
> "I do," Alice hastily replied; "at least—at least I mean what I say—that's the same thing, you know."
>
> "Not the same thing a bit!" said the Hatter. "Why, you might just as well say that 'I see what I eat' is the same thing as 'I eat what I see!'"
>
> -Lewis Carroll
> *Alice's Adventures in Wonderland*

RED HERRING The name of this fallacy has an interesting background: In order to keep fox hunters and their hounds from running through their crops, English farmers would drag a strong-smelling red herring along the edge of their fields. The farmers threw the dogs off track by presenting a smell that was stronger than the scent of the fox.

A red herring used in argumentation introduces an irrelevant issue in order to divert attention from the real subject at hand. For example:

> *It's ridiculous to worry about cleaning up our country's polluted waters when so many innocent people are being killed by international terrorists.*

> *Why should we worry about increasing violence in video games when thousands of people are injured in automobile accidents every day?*

> *We can't spend our time discussing graduation standards when there is so much racial tension in the school.*

BANDWAGON Bandwagon assumes that because something is popular, it is therefore good or desirable. A great deal of advertising depends on the bandwagon fallacy. Consider this example:

> *More people use _____ pain reliever than any other.*

The fact that more people use one kind of pain reliever does not prove that it is a better pain reliever. Its popularity could be due to more aggressive advertising, not because it relieves pain better.

> *The President must be correct in his current foreign policy; after all, he has a 70 percent approval rating.*

The only way to determine if the President is correct in his foreign policy is to examine his policy in relation to its results. Popular opinion cannot prove that an idea is right or wrong.

EITHER-OR *Either-or* forces people to choose between two alternatives when more than two alternatives may exist. For instance:

> *Since there is no evidence, the crime did not occur.*

> *The government must either raise taxes or do away with Social Security.*

Each of these statements oversimplifies a complex issue by reducing it to a single choice. A critical listener might ask about the second example, *What about cutting benefits but not eliminating them? What about downsizing some other federal programs first?*

[W]e must be able to employ persuasion, just as strict reasoning can be employed, on opposite sides of a question, not in order that we may in practice employ it in both ways (for we must not make people believe what is wrong), but in order that we may see clearly what the facts are, and that, if another man argues unfairly, we on our part may be able to confute him.

-Aristotle

Always ask yourself if there are other choices.

> *Mom, would you rather buy me a new pair of shoes or pay for my tongue piercing?*

Mom also has a third choice. Before you accept one alternative in an either/or argument, make certain that you are not missing other options.

EMOTIONAL APPEAL Emotional appeals, which Aristotle referred to more than 2,000 years ago in his book, *Rhetoric*,[2] are intended to persuade— through sadness, anger, guilt, fear, happiness, pride, sympathy, reverence, and other emotions. Although it is a valid technique in persuasion, emotional appeal can sometimes pack too much emotion and weaken the overall impact.

> *When persuasion is the end, passion also must be engaged.*
>
> -Aristotle

The following examples pack too much emotion:

> *This defendant deserves a light sentence due to the impoverished circumstances of his upbringing.*

> *Any man who drives a car like this one is a real man. You certainly belong in this car!*

Be careful not to substitute emotional appeal for sound evidence and sound reasoning. You must first prove your case; only then is it effective to add emotion to stir your audience on to belief or action.

CIRCULAR REASONING Circular reasoning argues in a circle—it ends up at the same place it started.

> *Dieting is good for you because it cuts down on the food you eat.*

> *I believe my friend is telling the truth because he says he's telling the truth.*

> *Using drugs should not be legal because if there wasn't anything wrong with it, it would already be legal, which it isn't.*

> *Your choice of available choices right now is limitless.* (advertisement in front of a store)

> *Always go to other people's funerals, otherwise they won't come to yours.*
>
> -Yogi Berra

As you can see, circular reasoning gets you nowhere. We cannot expect someone to accept a controversial claim based upon premises that are just as controversial. Remember to dig further for more facts if you find yourself (or someone else) using circular reasoning.

---

[2] Aristotle's *Rhetoric* is a classic work on the methods of persuasion. You can access the full text of this book on the World Wide Web at http://classics.mit.edu/Aristotle/rhetoric.html.

Academic Argumentation

Reason is the substance of the universe, the design of the world is absolutely rational.

-Hegel

Once you've learned to reason logically in everyday argumentation, you can apply the same concepts to your academic assignments. Good argumentation plays a major role in essays, research papers, speeches, and basic problem solving. Academic argumentation is essentially taking a scholarly position, defending it reasonably, and attempting to persuade your audience.

Suppose the following question shaped your thesis statement on an assigned paper: *Was Benedict Arnold a traitor or, as he believed, a true American patriot?* In a persuasive academic argument like this, you would need to show the different points of view that give rise to the controversy (see Step 1 in the following chart). Then you would have to formulate your own point of view in order to answer the question at issue (see Step 2 in the chart). Your answer then becomes your thesis.

Take a close look at the next two charts to see how persuasive argumentation can be accomplished by using all the elements of thought involved in critical thinking.

Step 1 (Compares Three Points of View)

Question at Issue: Was Benedict Arnold a traitor or, as he believed, a true American patriot?

POINT OF VIEW	Benedict Arnold	The American Colonists	The British
PURPOSE	To win the war	To secure independence	To maintain control of colonies
QUESTION AT ISSUE	How to fight successfully	How to rid the colonies of British dominance	How to secure control of rebels
EVIDENCE (DATA)	Benedict Arnold was a hero at Saratoga and elsewhere. His ideas were seen as "irregular." Tide of war seemed to be turning toward British. Soldiers were cold and ill-fed; they were more farmers than soldiers. Arnold changed sides. He accepted 10,000 pounds for the colonists' plans.	Colonists were victors at Saratoga. Determined leadership in spite of physical and emotional hardships.	British lost at Saratoga. Had difficulty fighting a continent away. Saw Arnold as a potential ally. Offered money to Arnold for revolutionaries' plans.
CONCEPT	War Successful tactical operations	War Unconditional victory	Uprising to be quelled
ASSUMPTIONS	Colonies not fighting effectively. War going on too long. Colonists suffering, with no apparent chance for victory. If British had the colonists' plans, they could end the war and colonies could cut their losses and return to normal prosperity.	Victory will surely come if troops are patient. Patriots are protecting their homes. An opportunity to gain the advantage is at hand.	Americans are uncivilized. Their troops are raggle-taggle and yet devious. Arnold would help with cause. Loyalists are the "good guys."
CONCLUSION	Join the British forces. Win the war with those who know how to fight properly. Establish himself as a true American hero.	Fight the British until they retreat.	Quell the riots and illegal uprising any way possible.
CONSEQUENCE	Made choice to join British. Was forced to flee to England and live out his life in exile, disgraced and despondent.	Considered Arnold a traitor. Marked him forever as a model for treachery. Refused to allow him to return to America.	Accepted colonists' plans from Arnold, but not his tactics for winning the war. Provided Arnold asylum in England.

It's obvious from the chart that Benedict Arnold did not see himself as a traitor. It is also apparent that the American colonists did consider him a traitor and the British regarded him as their ally. Fill in the empty boxes on the following chart using your own point of view. Come up with your own conclusion on the issue.

Step 2 (Your Point of View)

Question at Issue: Was Benedict Arnold a traitor or, as he believed, a true American patriot?

	What to do	Your Answers
POINT OF VIEW	Look at everything from your own point of view.	My point of view
PURPOSE	Determine your purpose in this argument (Your purpose is satisfied in the consequence.).	
QUESTION AT ISSUE	Write out your question at issue (What is the problem to be solved?).	
EVIDENCE (DATA)	What are the known facts (no opinions yet)? Pick the data that you consider relevant from the table in Step 1.	
CONCEPT	Decide the context. (Will you use present standards or the standards of the Colonial Period?) You will also need to choose from the British concept (an uprising), the Colonial concept (a war demanding unconditional victory), or Arnold's concept (a war demanding successful tactical operations).	
ASSUMPTIONS	Make your own assumptions about Arnold, his position, your idea of the war, the Colonists' response, the British position, etc.	
CONCLUSION	Decide if Arnold acted appropriately or inappropriately. Take a stand and say "yes" or "no" to the question at issue. Your reasons must be based on your answers given above.	
CONSEQUENCE	Decide if Arnold's exile was or was not a fitting punishment. Then come up with your own consequence based on all the above elements of your own critical thinking.	

Summary

The reasoning involved in critical thinking is useful in all areas of thought and learning. It is especially practical, however, when used in argumentation, or the art of persuasion. With powerful argumentation skills, you can make a claim, support it with reliable evidence, and come up with a logical, strong conclusion.

Your evidence, however, will be ineffective unless you link it to the proper rationale—the reasoned connection—which is the key to persuasion. This chapter covers four general categories of rationales. With inductive generalization, you move from a number of particular facts to a general conclusion. A deductive generalization works in reverse—you move from a general premise to a particular conclusion. When you use causal reasoning, you support your claim by proving cause and effect. In analogic reasoning, you compare situations that are parallel in structure and assume that what is true for the one is also true for the other.

No matter what kind of reasoning you use, you will want to avoid the potential fallacies, or errors in reasoning, that often accompany rationales. Inductive and deductive generalizations can become hasty generalizations when you jump to conclusions on the basis of insufficient or skewed evidence.

When showing cause and effect, it is sometimes easy to base your conclusion on false cause—assuming incorrectly that one event caused another. Also be aware of invalid analogies when you assume that two situations are essentially alike. Some other fallacies to watch out for include *ad hominem*, red herring, bandwagon, either-or, emotional appeal, and circular reasoning.

Applying good argumentation techniques to your academic assignments, as well as to all other aspects of your life, will give you confidence in what you say, what you write, and what you believe. When you support your convictions with sound evidence and complete analysis, your conclusions are well thought out and based on critical thinking.

By using the art of persuasion, you will find that other people will often be convinced to adopt your point of view as they understand the reliable logic behind your thinking. By being aware of the strengths of sound persuasion, you will be less apt to become the victim of someone else's unsound, flawed reasoning.

Let's Talk

1. Is it possible to have argumentation without persuasion? Explain your answer. Is it possible to have persuasion without argumentation? Explain your answer.

2. Explain how claim, evidence, and rationale directly relate to the elements of thought in the process of critical thinking.

3. Identify any fallacies that are present in the following passages (there may be more than one in each passage):

   (1) The number of football players that abuse drugs is creating a widespread, critical problem. Three players from one professional team admitted last week that they had used cocaine.

   (2) The IRS never goes after the big corporations, just the little guy like you and me. I was audited last year, and my friend was audited the year before. Ever hear of Exxon getting nailed? Just what do you think their profits were last year?

Apply the Concepts

1. Suppose you are in this situation: *Dr. Schapiro gave you a "C" on your paper because she does not agree with your opinion. It makes you angry because you believe your opinion is just as valid as hers.* Since it would be unproductive for you to meet with Dr. Schapiro just to argue opinions, explain in detail how you would prepare to support your opinion logically before you talk to her.

2. In the following paragraph, identify: (1) the claim, (2) the evidence supporting the claim, (3) the rationale used in the argument, and (4) any fallacies that exist.

   The school year for students in grades K–12 should be extended to include the summer. The teachers will be paid for an additional two months. Students will be exposed to more material. Curriculum will be covered in more depth and students will have more opportunities to practice their new skills. With more time spent and more information obtained, students will gain a deeper understanding of the material. As a result, America's public schools will be producing young adults who are better prepared to meet the demands of the working world.

3. Using the Benedict Arnold charts on pages 205–206, write an argumentative essay, persuading the reader to adopt your conclusion on the issue. If you have not done so, you must first complete the chart on page 206 to determine your own point of view.

4. From the list below, choose one claim that you accept. Take about twenty minutes to write an essay defending your position and persuading others to adopt your claim. Be sure to use all the elements of argumentation to prove your claim. Now write your name on the back of the paper. On a separate sheet of paper, write down a number from 1 to 10 to grade yourself on the strength of your argument (10 = very strong; 1 = very weak).

The very wealthy pay less in taxes than they should.	Welfare makes people lazy.
Rap music contributes to the crime problem.	Nice guys finish last.
Chocolate causes acne.	Spare the rod and spoil the child.
Women are more gentle and nurturing than men.	You get what you pay for.
The death penalty is a deterrent to murder.	Vitamin C prevents colds.
The death penalty is not a deterrent to murder.	Politicians are untrustworthy.

When everyone is finished, the instructor will collect the papers and redistribute them to the class. In groups of three or four, read the papers and assign each one a "grade" from 1 to 10 (10 = very strong; 1 = very weak). When the groups are finished, the instructor will return the papers to their authors. When you get yours back, compare the "grade" you gave yourself to the "grade" given by the group that read your paper. The instructor may ask volunteers to defend their own judgment of their argument against the judgment of the group. Be ready to defend your paper and the grade you gave yourself.

13
GOOD WRITING—
A Product of
Critical Thinking

The Power of the Written Word

The Elements of Critical Writing

Becoming Your Own Editor

Documentation and Attribution

Summary

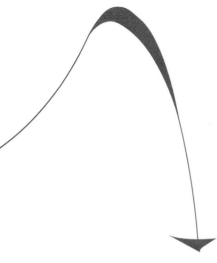

You've come a long way in your critical thinking process. From a thorough analysis of the elements of thought, you've explored argument, rationales, fallacies, academic argumentation, and persuasion. If you're taking advantage of these aspects of critical thinking, you're no doubt enjoying the ability to reason with confidence and persuade others in academic and other situations.

In this chapter, you will advance to the art of good writing—the ability to translate your critical thinking into effective written expression.

The Power of the Written Word

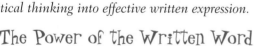

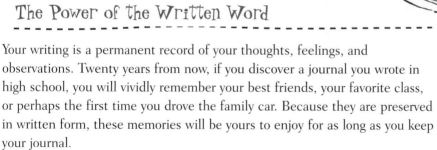

Your writing is a permanent record of your thoughts, feelings, and observations. Twenty years from now, if you discover a journal you wrote in high school, you will vividly remember your best friends, your favorite class, or perhaps the first time you drove the family car. Because they are preserved in written form, these memories will be yours to enjoy for as long as you keep your journal.

On a practical level, effective writing is your passport to academic achievement and professional accomplishment. There are numerous careers for someone who writes professionally—novelist, nonfiction writer, technical

Nothing has really happened until it has been recorded.

-Virginia Woolf

Either write something worth reading or do something worth writing.

-Benjamin Franklin

writer, advertising copywriter, Webmaster, newspaper reporter, television writer, to name a few.

Good writing is a prerequisite for countless other professions as well. Scientists write understandable research reports; lawyers write convincing briefs and persuasive legal arguments; judges write clear opinions that set important legal precedents; and legislators write laws that effectively guide local and national government. Historians record valuable information for future generations, while corporate managers and their staffs communicate effectively in written memos, letters, e-mail, and reports. All these people are motivated to write in order to accomplish the essentials of their chosen fields.

Writing is a strenuous mental activity that requires motivation. Students are often motivated to write in order to complete assignments and meet deadlines. If you look at the "big picture"—your entire future—you'll see the far-reaching rewards of good writing. Your ability to write well will put you an academic step ahead and will help you excel in the career of your choice.

The Elements of Critical Writing

Now that you're equipped with the foundations of critical thinking, you're ready to master effective writing by transferring those strategies to the written page. In any academic setting (from elementary to graduate school), you are frequently required to write down your thoughts in a variety of forms. You may be asked to write a short answer on a test, brief answers to chapter questions, short **essays**, long essays, or research papers. As you've probably noticed, the purpose of your writing has shifted significantly as you've advanced to higher levels of education. Perhaps you've moved from a focus on expressing well-organized facts to a greater emphasis on proving a **thesis** or solving a problem.

In college, your focus will move to original research as you attempt to answer questions or mysteries that have not yet been resolved. Because you'll be investigating hypothetical situations, you probably won't know the answer to your question or the solution to your mystery until your research is well underway. The answer that emerges from your research is your thesis.

Never express yourself more clearly than you are able to think.

-Niels Bohr

History will be kind to me for I intend to write it.

-Sir Winston Churchill

essay
a short composition on a particular theme or subject

thesis
a position or proposition that a person proves or maintains by argument

Truth in science can be defined as the working hypothesis best suited to open the way to the next better one.

-Konrad Lorenz

RHETORICAL MODES In order to improve essays and research papers, many college students use what are called "rhetorical modes" (*rhetoric*: the art of using language effectively and persuasively, and *mode*: a particular form). These are sometimes referred to as "rhetorical forms" or "rhetorical devices." Simply put, a rhetorical mode is a form of writing that helps writers communicate effectively and persuasively. The chart on the next page shows some common rhetorical modes that students use to develop their academic writing. Notice how some of these modes have their origins in good argumentation and persuasion (see Chapter 12).

In ancient Athens, a group of teachers called Sophists used persuasive language to win arguments. Their brilliant use of words dazzled many Athenians who paid them well for their ability to persuade.

In addition to teaching, some Sophists took on odd jobs such as persuading reluctant dental patients to have a tooth pulled. Socrates called the Sophists "rhetoricians" and convinced his students that their talent with language, though showy, was no substitute for real reasoning.

Common Rhetorical Modes
in Academic Writing

Argumentation Assumes a position, then defends it with the best supporting evidence and rationale.

Example: It is worth going into debt to finance a college education because your annual income after graduation will greatly exceed that of non-graduates.

Cause/Effect Explains how one action triggers a reaction. Uses a case study to show how one action is responsible for the resulting effect.

Example: Students should be careful to borrow only the minimum amount necessary to finance a college education because debt payments will burden them during the years they are trying to establish careers and families.

Comparison and Contrast Discusses differences and similarities to reach a conclusion. (Works like a pro/con T-chart using written text instead of a graphic representation.)

Example: A dozen Ivy League graduates who had large debts for their college educations were compared to a dozen graduates of public colleges who had modest debts. The difference in their incomes for the first year after graduation was insignificant.

Definition Gives extended and specific meanings of words, phrases, or concepts. Essays about "the true meaning of the holiday season" or "what it means to be an American" fall into this category.

Example: Signing your name to a student loan contract means you will be assuming a financial burden for a specific number of years.

Example Gives specific examples to support the topic or thesis. If your thesis is, "Student loan repayments can overburden people in their early professional years," you should use examples of graduates who over-borrowed.

Example: Sylvia Green, a college graduate, weighed her job offers not on the basis of what would give her satisfaction, but on what would provide her with sufficient income to pay down her $18,000 student loan balance.

Persuasion Uses reason to convince readers or listeners to adopt the writer's belief or position. Although very similar to argumentation, persuasion has a more conciliatory tone.

Example: A high school senior should consider attending a local community college before transferring to a four-year college in order to avoid a huge debt after graduation.

Process Describes a procedure in detail, usually breaking it down into sequential parts. Technical writers use this mode to write instructions for a specific procedure.

Example: The procedure for borrowing money for college is complex and time consuming but ultimately worthwhile. Here's how to navigate your way through the process.

Remember: ~ Different rhetorical modes are suited to different purposes. The examples above show the many variations you can develop from the same data.

~ Rhetorical modes can be used for short or long writing assignments (from a single paragraph to a fully developed research paper).

The particular rhetorical mode you choose will depend on the purpose of your writing at a given time. For instance, if a technical writer wants to explain how to use a software program, the *process mode* would be the most effective method of communication. If you were asked to participate in a debate on whether Social Security benefits for your age group should be funded with public or private investments, the *comparison mode* would be your best choice.

In more complex writing assignments such as a research paper, you are not limited to one rhetorical mode. For example, in a paper about the Social Security funding issue, your primary rhetorical mode might be the *comparison mode*, but you would most likely support it with the *definition mode* and the *example mode*.

MANAGING THE PROCESS A long writing assignment can seem like an impossible task unless you effectively manage the process. The task management techniques in Chapter 6 work well with lengthy writing assignments. A research paper typically involves research, documentation, creativity, word processing, and careful writing. In college, a research paper is usually assigned three or four months before the due date, or at the beginning of the college term.

Once you know what your assignment is, you'll need to break it down into smaller, more manageable tasks. This not only makes your job easier but gives you time to clarify your ideas and conclusions.

The process you use to get the assignment done will be uniquely your own. Since students have their own learning styles and right-brain/left-brain tendencies, processes will vary among students for the same assignment. The important thing is that you manage your tasks well to meet the deadline.

Once your assignment is divided into manageable tasks, your next step is to assign target deadlines to each task. Look at the following example of a college research paper assignment that is due at the end of the term. Notice how the assignment is divided into 14 weeks to complete all tasks. Remember, though, that this is only a plan. Research may take a shorter or longer time to reveal sound conclusions, so the plan will need to be adjusted as the paper progresses. The schedule may at first seem overwhelming, but keep in mind that some of the tasks will only take a short amount of time.

Managing the Process—a Sample

Research Paper — 14 Weeks

Assignment: Write a 15-page paper on Henry David Thoreau and his experiment at Walden Pond. You have 14 weeks to complete the assignment.

Week 1	Week 2	Week 3	Week 4
~ Read *Walden*. Check out other books by and about Thoreau. Begin your study. When a passage stands out to you, copy it (with full reference) onto an index card or enter it on a computer	~ Think about ideas and themes that are emerging. Write down questions you have about Thoreau's experiment. These are called **Shaping Questions**. ***Examples of Shaping Questions*** ~ *Did extreme frugality really enrich Thoreau's life?* ~ *What was so attractive to Thoreau about the simple life?* ~ *Could Thoreau's experiment have been successful in a city, or were isolation and nature essential requirements?* ~ Continue your reading, copying, and referencing.	~ Choose the **Shaping Question** that is most interesting to you. ~ Use key words about Thoreau and his experiment to do an Internet search. Find out all you can about Walden Pond and the tiny cabin he built there. ~ Suppose the shaping question that produces the greatest number of sources and intrigues you most is: *Could Thoreau's experiment have been successful in a city, or were isolation and nature essential requirements?* This will become your focus.	~ Continue your reading, paying close attention to any information relevant to your shaping question.

Week 5	Week 6	Week 7	Weeks 8 and 9
~ If possible, visit a park or pond that will give you a sense of Thoreau's solitude and experiences. Imagine how he felt (by now, you already know a lot about what he thought).	~ After reading and reflecting, your answer to the shaping question becomes: *Thoreau's experiment in simplicity could only have been successful in an isolated natural setting with no urban distractions.* This answer becomes your **Thesis**. ~ Spread out your index cards and/or print out all your research notes. Write the first draft of your first page (the Introduction). Include citations that support your claims.	~ Go to the library or search the Internet to find out if any letters by Thoreau have been published or preserved. ~ Do some reading on other Transcendentalists such as Ralph Waldo Emerson. What did they think of Thoreau and his experiment? Take relevant notes.	~ Continue writing your rough draft. Your goal for Week 8: finish page 5. Your goal for Week 9: finish page 9.

Week 10	Weeks 11 and 12	Week 13	Week 14
~ Answer these questions: *Have I met at least the minimum requirement for the number of sources? Are my sources appropriate, credible, and scholarly?* ~ Continue reading source material and select the statements that most strongly support your thesis. ~ Continue writing your rough draft. Your goal: finish page 12.	~ Complete your rough draft. ~ Add your bibliography or works cited page. ~ Make sure your bibliography or works cited page and your footnotes or endnotes match your teacher's style requirement (such as MLA or APA style).	~ Return books to the library. Take a complete break from your paper.	~ Read your entire paper. ~ Revise if necessary to make it more convincing. ~ Look for errors and correct them. Run spell-check and grammar-check programs. Make any changes you wish. ~ Turn in your paper. ~ CELEBRATE!

Now that you've seen one example of how to manage a large writing assignment, let's take a look at the parts that make up the process.

BEGINNING YOUR PAPER If you've been given no limitations on the topic you can choose, then focus on what interests you most. *What subject really fascinates me? Is there a question I'd like to answer? Is there an issue I'd like to prove or a mystery I'd like to solve?* If you're limited to the subject matter in a particular discipline, ask yourself what intrigues you about that particular field or what issue you'd like to investigate. Then narrow your interests to a specific topic.

Your topic may be something you already know a lot about. Prior knowledge about a subject will give you the freedom to explore a specific aspect of it in more depth. On the other hand, your subject may be something you know little about, making it a learning experience for you. You may also want to explore a very controversial topic, standing firm in the conclusion you reach after you've thoroughly researched the issue.

PRELIMINARY RESEARCH Let's say that you choose Edgar Allan Poe as your topic. Next, you will need to do some preliminary reading and research on Poe in order to determine what ideas or themes emerge for you. Write down any questions that you have about Poe as you do your research. These are your shaping questions.

Next, look for answers to your shaping questions. You may want to do a subject-based search on the Internet as a brainstorming aid when you answer your questions. Linking to subtopics will help you find interesting and relevant facts from which you can formulate conclusions that will eventually shape your thesis.

I find that a great part of the information I have was acquired by looking up something and finding something else on the way.

-Franklin P. Adams

THE SHAPING QUESTION Following is an actual case history that illustrates how to form a creative shaping question. In this example, the broad topic is Edgar Allan Poe, but the shaping question directs the subject to an actual mystery or issue that needs to be solved. You'll use critical thinking strategies to sort and work through the mystery or question at hand.

Choosing A Shaping Question

Sid Newbold, a sophomore at Hudson Valley Community College, enjoyed the horror stories of Edgar Allan Poe. He felt that Poe was a precursor of modern writers such as Stephen King. Because of his interest in the author's writing and life, Sid decided that his research paper would focus on a little-known aspect of Poe's life.

Sid read in a biography that Poe probably died from liver damage typical of alcoholism, although the official cause of his death in 1849 was recorded as "congestion of the brain." While searching the Internet, Sid came across a bizarre theory that he'd never heard before—that Poe actually died of rabies. Although it sounded rather far fetched, Sid read the complete account on the Web page and became even more intrigued.

He then asked his teacher if he could make this enigma the basis for his required research paper. He argued, "It's like an episode of the television show *ER*, only it happened more than 150 years ago." His teacher approved his thesis statement, reminding him to credit his Internet source in the final paper. Thus, Sid wrote a shaping question in defense of his plan: Did Poe die of rabies or advanced liver damage from alcoholism?

Now let's relate Sid's shaping question to the elements of thought (see Chapter 11).

Point of View:	*Sid's*
Purpose:	*To determine whether Poe's death was a direct result of alcoholism or rabies.*
Question at Issue	
(Shaping Question):	*Did Poe die from rabies or advanced liver damage from alcoholism?*
Thesis Statement:	*(Still unknown)*

With sound preliminary research and an interesting shaping question, you're ready to gather evidence.

The concept is interesting and well-formed, but in order to earn better than a "C", the idea must be feasible.

-Yale University management professor in response to student Fred Smith's paper proposing reliable overnight delivery service (Smith went on to found Federal Express Corp.)

GATHERING EVIDENCE Many sources are available as you gather evidence to answer your shaping question. You can use the library by searching for relevant books, magazine articles, newspaper articles, and reference material (published letters, quotation books,[1] and biographical aids.[2]) In addition, you can write, e-mail, or call organizations that have information on your subject and provide information to the public. You might also find someone you can interview who has specialized knowledge in your given topic. Sometimes your own experience even turns out to be a good resource.

EVALUATE YOUR SOURCES The Internet, of course, provides a huge storehouse of information on almost any subject. It's an excellent resource if you use it responsibly. Since anyone with a computer and Internet access can put things on the Internet, it is important to evaluate the source before you use the information. First, make sure the Web document is up-to-date by checking the last date of revision, if it is available. It's also important to find out if the Web page was written by a reliable, credible source. If the document was produced by an organization, you will have to judge whether that organization is impartial and scholarly enough to cite in your paper. You may have to do some additional research on the author or the organization before you use the information. If you cannot confirm the credentials or identity of a Web page's author, you should probably look for a better source.

KEEP TRACK OF REFERENCES As you research and take notes, be sure to keep a preliminary bibliography or works cited page either on index cards or on the computer. To save yourself some time, you may want to assign a number or a key word to each one of your sources. Each time you use a source in your notes or your rough draft, just jot down the number or the key word next to the information. When you finalize the paper, you can insert the complete reference to the source. Some word-processing programs will automatically sort and format sources for you, making your task easier, but make sure its style agrees with your assignment. (See page 233.)

Now let's take a look at how Sid gathered data in support of his claim about the death of Edgar Allan Poe.

---

[1] The best-known collection of quotations is *Bartlett's Familiar Quotations*. Other excellent quotation books include: *Oxford Dictionary of Quotations*; and *Harper Book of American Quotations*.

[2] Biographical aids are books that contain brief life and career facts about contemporary men and women. Some of the ones you may find most useful include: *International Who's Who; Who's Who in America; Who's Who of American Women*.

Researching For Evidence

Sid began collecting everything he could find on Poe's death. His mission at this point was not to prove that his rabies theory was correct, but to see what, in general, the evidence had to say.

Sid found out that Poe died on October 7, 1849. He also discovered that Poe had been found unconscious on a public park bench in Baltimore. Though there was no evidence of trauma and no smell of alcohol on his breath, Poe had experienced some hallucinations, a headache, and some nausea. In addition, Sid learned that Poe refused alcohol for six months prior to entering the hospital and had trouble drinking water once he was admitted. His pupils were dilating and contracting, and he became "combative and had to be restrained."

Most of Poe's contemporaries assumed that liver damage was the cause of his death because Poe was known to use alcohol heavily. However, the week of his death, Poe was scheduled to be remarried, which would lead people to believe that he would refrain from excessive drinking in order to be healthy and well for this occasion.

In the course of further research, Sid unexpectedly found there were plausible opportunities for Poe to have been bitten by a rabid animal. To Sid's surprise, he learned that the symptoms of terminal liver damage and advanced rabies are similar. He also read that a period of time may elapse between being bitten by a rabid animal and the onset of rabies symptoms. Finally, Sid discovered that, according to Poe's friends, Poe had not consumed any alcohol for six months.

At this point, Sid had enough information to write the introduction and begin drafting his paper. As you begin to write your paper, remember that the first part must lay a good foundation of facts and background information in order to set the stage for the argument.

Graphic organizers are valuable tools at this stage of your writing (see Chapter 9). You may find it helpful to place your facts on a time line or some other linear array. If your shaping question involves cause and effect, you may want to create a flowchart. If you are answering a question with a *yes* or *no* answer, then a pro/con T-chart works well. In Sid's case, he had two options for his shaping question: (a) *Did Poe die of rabies?* or (b) *Did Poe die of liver damage from alcoholism?* Sid used a comparison T-chart to determine the strengths and weaknesses of the two sides of his issue.

Sid's Comparison T-Chart

Sid decided to construct a comparison T-chart to determine whether the evidence tipped the argument in favor of the rabies theory or the alcohol-related death theory. This is how Sid's T-chart looked:

Thesis: *Did Poe die of rabies or advanced liver damage from alcoholism?*

RABIES	ALCOHOL-RELATED
1. Pupil dilation and contraction	1. History of alcohol abuse
2. Chances for exposure to rabid animals	2. Exposure to rabies undocumented
3. Agitation, hallucination, nausea	3. Can occur with other illnesses
4. Unable to drink water (typical of rabies)	4. Can occur with other illnesses
5. Drank no alcohol for 6 months; refused alcohol in hospital	5. Damage to liver may have already occurred
6. Poe engaged; good reason to not drink	6. His lifelong behavior patterns were erratic
7. Attending physician revised diagnosis; later suggested rabies more plausible	7. "Congestion of the brain" was diagnosis at time of death
8. Modern physician reviewed symptoms; said rabies was likely	8. No known laboratory evidence survives

RATIONALES AND ASSUMPTIONS As you understand the relationships and concepts of your data, you will naturally employ rationales and assumptions. By using the comparison T-chart, Sid actually made some assumptions as he moved from particular facts to a general conclusion.

In comparing the two sides of his argument, Sid no doubt hoped to determine which side was stronger. At this point, however, both sides seemed equally convincing. As he moved on to write some more of his paper, Sid realized that his research would not likely culminate in the decisive conclusion he had originally expected.

There is no good arguing with the inevitable. The only argument available with an east wind is to put on your overcoat.

-James Russell Lowell

THESIS STATEMENT Sid first determined that his facts did not completely answer his shaping question. He found there was plenty of good evidence to support both the rabies theory and the alcohol theory, and thus, he could not completely prove his theory conclusively. Since Sid used inductive generalization as his rationale, he had to be careful not to make any hasty generalizations. Rather than distort the facts to fit his purpose, Sid decided to write a thesis statement that was somewhat different from what he first expected.

Although the facts did not prove it, they did make a case that Poe *could* have died of undiagnosed rabies. Consequently, Sid wrote his **thesis statement** to read as follows:

> *Though Edgar Allan Poe was presumed by many to have died of alcohol-related liver damage, a workable case could be made that he died of undiagnosed rabies.*

CONCLUSION Sid's thesis statement was not as sweeping as the initial theory he set out to prove, but it was verifiable. A logical consequence of his research might have read something like this:

> *Because of this research paper, many will consider the possibility that Edgar Allan Poe could have died as a result of rabies, not alcohol-related liver damage. Most will at least think of Poe's last days and death in a different way.*

It is important to note that Sid did not determine a definitive thesis statement and conclusion until he evaluated most of the information and evidence.

Once you've established your thesis statement and reached a conclusion, you can finish writing your paper. At this point, consider your paper a rough draft, not yet a completed assignment. In the next section, you will become your own editor, revising and polishing your draft to make it into a finished product.

Take a look at how far you've already come. The chart on the next page, which uses Sid's research paper as an example, shows how the writing process corresponds to the critical thinking process you've been learning about in the first twelve chapters. Compare Sid's steps to the elements of thought in Chapter 11.

> The great tragedy of Science—the slaying of a beautiful hypothesis by an ugly fact.
>
> -Thomas Henry Huxley

> The folly of mistaking a paradox for a discovery, a metaphor for a proof, a torrent of verbiage for a spring of capital truths, and oneself for an oracle, is inborn in us.
>
> -Paul Valery

Critical Writing is Thinking Critically

Point of View	Sid's
Purpose	To determine whether Poe's death was a direct result of alcoholism or rabies.
Question at Issue (Shaping Question)	Though Edgar Allan Poe was presumed by many to die of alcohol-related liver damage, does the evidence show that he could have died of undiagnosed rabies?
Evidence	Research (verifiable facts and rationale)
Concept	A comparison T-chart showed that there was evidence to support the theory that Poe may have died of rabies. There was also evidence to support the theory that Poe died of alcohol-related liver damage.
Rationales/ Assumptions	Sid assumed that Poe could have died as a result of rabies. He found that the same rationale showed that Poe also could have died from liver damage.
Conclusion (Thesis Statement)	Though Edgar Allan Poe was presumed by many to die of alcohol-related liver damage, a workable case could be made that he died of undiagnosed rabies.
Consequence	Because of this research paper, many will consider the possibility that Edgar Allan Poe could have died as a result of rabies, not alcohol-related liver damage. Most will at least think of Poe's last days and death in a different way.

Becoming Your Own Editor

Some students have no trouble when it comes to topic, shaping questions, research, assumptions, and thesis statement. However, when it comes time to write a paper with sound sentence structure, smooth transitions, and grammatical accuracy, some students don't do very well.

If doubts about grammar and structure sometimes slow you down or weaken your writing, then this section is for you. If you happen to have a good grasp on the grammatical elements of writing, then you will appreciate some of the new self-editing techniques in this part.

REVISING YOUR ROUGH DRAFT Before you take the time to correct grammatical errors, you should read over your rough draft. Imagine that you are no longer the writer; you are now the reader who is seeing the material for the first time. In essence, you will become your own editor. As you read, ask yourself questions like, *Does this make sense to me? Would I understand this without any background knowledge? Is it interesting? Is it logical?*

If your answer to any of these questions is *No*, you will have a good clue as to the way you should change the text. You may have to clarify your facts, explain your rationale better, make your sentences more appealing, or improve your transitions. The following four writing elements (or characteristics) will improve your sentences and the overall quality of your writing—*voice*, *tone*, *balance*, and *pace*.

With a pencil and paper, I could revise the world.

-Alison Lurie

Voice

EXPLANATION

In writing, voice refers to who or what is doing the action of the verb. There are two voices—**active** and **passive**.

In the active voice, the subject (who or what does the action of the verb) is usually a person, a group of people, or a living thing. Most often, instructors and writing professionals prefer the active voice.

On the other hand, passive voice is often preferred in the sciences where observed date are emphasized rather than the person doing the observing.

EXAMPLES

Active Voice: Einstein formulated the Theory of Relativity.
Passive Voice: The Theory of Relativity was formulated by Einstein.

Active Voice: The New York Knicks lost the game.
Passive Voice: The game was lost by the New York Knicks.

Active Voice: The traffic court judge hears cases every Tuesday evening.
Passive Voice: Traffic cases are heard by the judge every Tuesday evening.

Remember: Avoid using both active and passive voice in one writing assignment. Shifting back and forth between voices can cause your writing to be confusing and irregular to the reader.

Tone

tone
style or manner of
expression in writing

Explanation

In music, tone refers to the quality of a sound (harsh, mellow). In art, tone is the quality or overall effect of the colors, tints, and shading. In writing, tone elicits a quality or overall effect. Through words, a writer expresses a certain mood or emotion. A writer's tone can be serious, humorous, ironic, supernatural, whimsical, haunting, reminiscent, defiant, and so on.

Examples

In the novel *To Kill a Mockingbird* by Harper Lee, the author creates a reflective tone by telling the story through the thoughts and recollections of a young girl named Scout. The author also creates a haunting tone as the reader shares in the fears that the children experience in their small southern town and the tragedy that unfolds there.

In the autobiography *Lakota Woman* by Mary Crow Dog, the reader gets an intense look into the mind of a Sioux woman. The tone is determined and sometimes rebellious.

Remember

As you can see from the examples, more than one tone can be present in a longer work like a book. However, you will be better off using just one tone in a shorter writing assignment.

Experiment with your own individual tone. Especially in creative writing assignments, try to capture your own or your characters' attitudes, experiences, and viewpoints.

Balance

balance
the construction of equal or parallel structures within a sentence or paragraph

Explanation

Balance refers to keeping your writing structures parallel—arranging two or more related words, phrases, or sentences in the same way.

Balance also refers to making the parts of a longer paper equal in importance and the length of each part appropriate to its importance.

Examples of Balanced Word Forms

My work was *too obscure, too symbolic,* and *too intellectual.* (Annie Dillard, *The Writing Life*)

To be or not *to be,* that is the question. (William Shakespeare, *Hamlet*)

Examples of Balanced Sentences

I know that when I am most monstrous, I am most in need of love. (Madeleine L'Engle, *The Irrational Season*)

They moved to Paris in 1958; they would remain there fifteen years. (Willie Morris, *James Jones: A Friendship*)

Example of a Balanced Paper

Introduction: *Though many presumed that Edgar Allan Poe died of alcohol-related liver damage, the evidence shows that he could have died of undiagnosed rabies.* (150 words)

  I. *Poe had a history of alcoholism.* (250 words)

  II. *Chances are Poe was exposed to rabies.* (200 words)

  III. *Death from rabies and death from alcohol-related liver damage are similar.* (220 words)

  IV. *There is evidence to support both theories on Poe's death.* (300 words)

Conclusion: *Though Poe was presumed to have died of alcohol-related liver damage, there is sufficient evidence to believe that he could have died from rabies.* (150 words)

Remember: A pair or a series of words in a sentence should be the same in structure. For example, if two words in a series end in "*ing,*" then the related ones should too.

Phrases and sentences that are related or next to each other should be parallel in structure.

Pace

Explanation

Pace is basically how fast new information is introduced in a piece of writing. In shorter essays, pacing is not usually an issue, but in longer papers and creative writing projects, pace is important.

Well-paced writing can provide the momentum necessary to keep your reader interested.

Tips For Well-Paced Writing

Say things once. Saying things in several different ways creates a kind of "echo" and slows down the pace of your paper. If you're just trying to make your paper longer, then search for more information, which is a better option than making your writing repetitive.

Weigh your words. Don't use too many descriptive words or too many words with three syllables or more. Be sure your sentences are easily understood.

> **Wordy:** *The efficacy of hydrochloric acid is indisputable, but the corrosive effect is incompatible with metallic permanence.*
>
> **Better:** *Don't use hydrochloric acid to clean out your drain. It eats holes in the pipes.*

Use action verbs. If you have a choice between a state-of-being verb (derivatives of "to be") and an action verb, choose the verb that shows action.

Use active voice. In the active voice, a subject performs the action of the verb. This gives more life to the text. (Note: Some computer grammar checks will highlight passive voice sentences as grammatical errors.)

Avoid tangents. Stick to your outline. When you start to digress, or go off on a tangent, ask yourself if the extra language is necessary, if it will engage your reader's attention, or if it will cause boredom.

Remember: You want to keep the interest of your reader.

There are no set formulas or rules for pacing your writing. You will have to use self-assessment to determine if your writing is "below or above the speed limit."

> Timing is everything. It is as important to know when as it is to know how.
>
> -Arnold Glasgow

You may also want someone else to read your paper. Feedback from a family member or a friend will show you from a less-biased source where your writing is unclear or weak.

BECOMING YOUR OWN PROOFREADER Once your rough draft reads well, you will need to check it for correct spelling and grammar. With the help of a few effective editing techniques, you can become your own custom proofreader.

If you've written your paper on a computer, which most instructors require you to do, be sure to use the spell-check and grammar-check tools in your word processing program first. They are useful as automatic correction tools as well as a type of tutorial to help you learn from your mistakes. Built-in thesaurus tools are also helpful when you're searching for just the right word or for some variety in your vocabulary.

Always be aware of certain errors that these program tools don't recognize—like the difference between "threw and through" or "to, too, and two." Most programs will not pick up the errors in sentences like these:

The to girls look like twins.
If you need some cash, my bank has a drive threw teller.

After using the computer's editing tools, you will still need to check your work for accuracy. Since we come to the writing process with a wide variety of educational backgrounds, your grammatical know-how might be much different from that of someone else in your class. You may be strong in one area of writing and weak in another. There may be just one kind of error that you habitually make, one that you just can't seem to get right. That's when a "Custom Proofreader's List" is helpful.

A Custom Proofreader's List is your own reminder of the writing errors you repeatedly make. In order to determine your most frequent errors, you will need to pay close attention to the mistakes that your instructors mark on your papers. You can also determine your common grammatical weaknesses from computer grammar checks or from your own knowledge—*The grammar check always catches my sentence fragments,* or *I always have trouble using "good" and "well" correctly.* Each time you have a writing assignment, your Custom Proofreader's List will be a good way to search for errors.

I am the Roman Emperor, and am above grammar.

-Emperor Sigismund

If a word in the dictionary were misspelled, how would we know?

-Steven Wright

Dew knot trussed yore spell chequer two fined awl yore mistakes.

-Brendan Hills

"Do you spell it with a 'V' or a 'W'?" inquired the judge.
"That depends upon the taste and fancy of the speller, my Lord."

-Charles Dickens

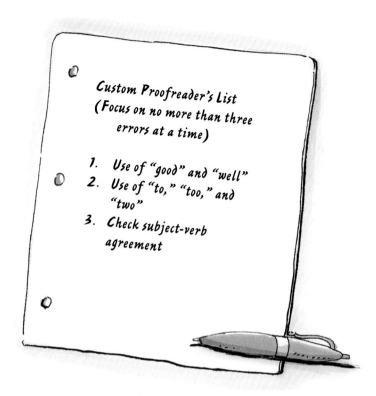

Custom Proofreader's List
(Focus on no more than three errors at a time)

1. Use of "good" and "well"
2. Use of "to," "too," and "two"
3. Check subject-verb agreement

Once you identify problems on your list, you will need to know how to correct them. You would benefit from purchasing a good grammar reference book for this purpose.[3]

Now you should read through your paper once for each type of potential error on your list. If you have three entries on your Custom Proofreader's List, you will read your paper a total of three times. If your list has on it the use of "to," "too," and "two," your first reading will be for that error only. Your second time through, you will look for one other type of error, and so on. Focusing on one specific problem at each reading will make it easier for you to spot your mistakes and correct them.

At this point, it would be a good idea to take one of your past papers and base your own Custom Proofreader's List on it. It will be helpful for you to find out right away what areas you need to work on so you're ready for your next paper.

The last step in the writing process is giving proper documentation and attribution to your sources.

[3] Good grammar reference books include the *Handbook for Writers*; *The Bedford Handbook*; and *Keys for Writers*, 2nd edition, by Ann Raimes, 1999. Well-known guidelines for writers include the *Chicago Manual of Style*, the *New York Times Stylebook*, the *American Psychological Association (APA) Stylebook*, and the *Associated Press Handbook*.

Documentation and Attribution

documentation
the providing of sources, usually in footnotes and bibliographies, for facts or statements made or hypotheses proposed

attribution
the crediting of specific words or ideas to a particular author or person

plagiarism
(from the Latin *plagium*, meaning "kidnapping.") passing off the words or ideas of someone else as your own

Adam was the only man who, when he said a good thing, knew that nobody said it before him.

-Mark Twain

In simple terms, **documentation** is showing from what source you got your facts. **Attribution** is making sure you give credit to others for the use of their words or ideas. When you fail to document a source or attribute language to someone else, you are guilty of **plagiarism**. At first, you may think that "guilty" is quite a strong term to use, but plagiarism does have serious consequences.

At some colleges, the consequences range from a failing grade to expulsion from the college to withholding of a degree. Keep in mind that there are many software programs and Web-built databases that make it easy for instructors or teaching assistants to check the originality of a student's work.

Professionals and politicians alike have been caught using parts of someone else's speech or written work, only to suffer a blemished reputation. Plagiarism is also against the law if a copyright or trademark is involved.

Let's go back to Sid Newbold's paper on the cause of Edgar Allan Poe's death. Sid got the idea for his thesis statement from an Internet source. The information on the Web page fascinated Sid, but he believed he could develop it further. As long as Sid credited his source, he could go forward ethically.

You might be wondering what ideas you can ever claim as your own. It's important to acknowledge that virtually all knowledge and writing builds on work that came before. For example, Galileo's theory of the universe was partly based upon the work of Copernicus. You, too, might learn from an expert, add your own thoughts and inspiration, and come up with a new theory or a different way to look at existing knowledge. Those ideas are indeed your own.

CREDITING YOUR SOURCES—DOCUMENTATION As you come to the end of your paper, you will need to credit your sources in footnotes, endnotes, a bibliography, or a works cited list. Keep in mind that a bibliography includes any sources you've used as background material for your paper—books, magazines and newspaper articles, reference material, Internet documents, interviews, films, videos, television programs, CD-ROM publications, and artwork. A works cited list includes only those sources from which you quoted directly in your paper.

As there are a number of bibliographical formats, you will need to check with your instructor to see what format you should follow. There are two major formats that are typically used—one devised by the Modern Language Association (MLA) and the other by the American Psychological Association (APA). Following are short-form references showing the basic formats for each of these two styles.

Bibliography Formats

MLA

Book

Author's last name, First name. Book Title. City: Publisher, date.

Periodical

Author's last name, First name. "Article Title." Periodical Title date: page numbers.

Online Entry

Author's last name, First name. "Title." Information on print version. Site title. Date posted or last updated. Sponsor. Date accessed <electronic address>.

APA

Book

Author's last name, Initial. (year). Book title. City: Publisher.

Periodical

Author's last name, Initial. (year, Month day). Article title. Periodical Title, pages.

Online Entry

Author's last name, Initial. (year, Month day). Title of article, chapter, or Web page [number of paragraphs]. Title of Full Work [on line], volume number. (issue number). Retrieved Month day year from source: electronic address

Note: Full-work titles may be underlined or, if you use a word-processor, italicized.

When you are actually preparing your citations, be sure to use a complete and up-to-date reference source for whichever form your instructor prefers. Comparing multiple examples is particularly helpful when you are trying to decide exactly where to put the punctuation and what information to include.

CREDITING YOUR SOURCES—ATTRIBUTION In order to explain attribution further, let's go back to Sid's paper. First, Sid needed to credit the author of the Web page where he got the idea for his thesis statement. As he gathered other sources, he would need to cite direct quotations, paraphrases, or ideas, most likely with footnotes, endnotes, or parenthetical notations.

Let's suppose that Sid used factual information from a 1998 book entitled *Midnight Dreary: The Mysterious Death of Edgar Allan Poe*. Also suppose that he sent an e-mail to the author, John Evangelist Walsh, and received a response. Any information Sid used from that e-mail communication would have to be attributed to Walsh. Let's say Sid went even further and called the author. Sid would also have to credit Walsh with any information he used from that phone interview.

You may well ask at this point, *If my paper is so full of documented and attributed material, what is left that is all mine?* Grammar expert Lynn Quitman Troyka gave an interesting answer to this question. She said that a student's original work typically consists of the thesis statement, the organizing sentences, the comments, the transitional sentences, and the summaries. Credit must be given for everything else.

An important aspect of your paper that belongs only to you is tone, or the personality of the creator expressed in writing. The way you present your paper, the evidence you use, the assumptions you make, and the conclusion belong to you alone. By making the quality of your language unique, the individuality of your writing will come through, no matter what kind of writing assignment you undertake.

It is amazing what you can accomplish if you do not care who gets the credit.

-Harry S. Truman

Summary

- -

The ability to write well improves your academic performance and helps you accomplish the written communication needed in your chosen career. To ignore good writing is to waste the chance to record your thoughts and ideas in a permanent, unambiguous form. The first twelve chapters of this course provided you with a firm foundation in critical thinking. These serve as the basis for good critical writing.

As you compare the elements of thought and argumentation to the elements of critical writing, you notice many similarities. Just the introduction in a research paper usually contains point of view, purpose, and a question at issue (shaping question). The body of the paper then logically follows with evidence, concepts established from data, and logical assumptions drawn through reasoning. The conclusion of a paper (thesis statement) answers the question at issue and describes the consequences as they relate to the purpose. If you train your mind to think critically, powerful writing should follow naturally.

Since your mind may often get jam-packed with scattered thoughts that only you can decipher, it's important to sharpen your writing and communication skills. What seems perfectly understandable to you may need thorough explanation on the written page. Having an excellent command of words and the ability to put them together correctly and clearly will give you an edge on effective written communication. It will put you a step ahead in your academic endeavors and in your chosen career.

The products of your mind—ideas, theories, solutions, opinions—will also improve your personal life. Your ability to think critically may help someone else or influence your community or even all of humanity. By writing down those products of your mind, you can permanently preserve them and share your ideas with the world.

What is conceived well is expressed clearly, and the words to say it will arrive with ease.

-Nicolas Boileau

There is one thing stronger than all the armies in the world, and that is an idea whose time has come.

-Victor Hugo

Let's Talk

1. Explain how you feel when you receive a writing assignment. (Describe in detail what aspects of writing you look forward to and which ones you dread.)

2. What advantages does a written communication have over an oral communication? Come up with some possible advantages that oral communications might have over written communications.

3. How are critical thinking, argumentation, and critical writing similar? How are they different?

4. Explain several reasons why task management is essential to the writing of research papers.

5. Explain the difference between preliminary research (before you determine your shaping question) and researching for evidence.

Apply the Concepts

1. Choose three topics from the following list (choose the topics with which you are most familiar). Write a shaping question for each topic.

AIDS	doctor-assisted suicide	juvenile murderers	school choice
airbags	drug laws	medical costs	school violence
alcohol abuse	genetic engineering	noise pollution	space exploration
child abuse	gun control	nuclear threat	water pollution
death penalty	hunger	poverty	Web censorship
DNA evidence	Internet security	road rage	wireless technology

2. Choose one of the shaping questions you wrote for question 1. Do an Internet search using key words that come to your mind. Write down several subtopics as you do your search. (Make a note of how many links you use to come up with suitable subtopics.) Choose one subtopic and follow the links further to come up with a more in-depth shaping question. Be prepared to share your results in class. The instructor may, at this point, ask your classmates to indicate whether they find the topic and/or shaping question interesting and what suggestions they have for the writer's approach to the topic.

3. Bring to class a copy of one of your recent, longer papers or writing assignments. Take your name off the paper. The instructor will collect the papers and redistribute them to the class, making sure no one gets his or her own paper. Your job is to edit someone else's paper by indicating in the margins where the content is unclear, illogical, or uninteresting. Be sure to edit for voice, tone, balance, and pace. Also check the elements of grammar such as spelling, punctuation, transitions, sentence fragments or run-ons. Finally, make suggestions for items on a personal proofreader's list. (After you get your paper back, your instructor may want you to meet with your "editor" to discuss the suggestions.)

4. Write a shortened version of a research paper based on all the elements in this chapter. To make research minimal, choose a topic with which you are very familiar. If you like, you can use one of the shaping questions you created in question 1. You may also use a current research assignment from another class, if you have one. (Check with your instructor if you will be using an assignment from another class so you can adjust your due date to correspond with the other assignment.) The importance of this assignment lies in your ability to write well using all the elements of critical thinking and critical writing.

Part 4
Independent Living—
Critical Thinking
for the Rest of Your Life

Critical Thinking in a Changing World

You might be wondering, *What more is there to learn about this critical thinking process? It seems as if we've covered just about everything.* There's no doubt that you have learned a lot and come a long way on your journey through *College Transition*. Take a quick look at the concepts you've examined.

You began by discovering your own powerful learning drive, that inborn quality that makes learning natural and fun. Then you learned about the amazing capabilities of your mind—the ability to develop patterns and concepts from an assortment of facts. From there, you moved on to hypotheses, analyses, sound judgments, and valid opinions.

Next, you discovered how to put all this mental capacity to work for you. Energized by internal motivation, you took control of your goals and your educational success. You became a self-regulated learner, using your critical thinking abilities to master class notes, reading material, and tests. Along the way, you became confident in your own learning style and also found out how you can adapt to other learning situations.

> Half this game is ninety percent mental.
> -Yogi Berra

Finally, after looking intensely at the elements of critical thinking, you progressed to persuasive argumentation and critical writing. If you're applying these first thirteen chapters to your educational life, then you're undoubtedly experiencing a higher level of academic achievement. You're also ready to tackle the scholastic demands of a college or university. Above all, you're prepared to deal with the many everyday challenges that will mark your path through college and beyond.

Living Independently—With Confidence

As you approach your college years, it's just as important to prepare for independent living as it is to prepare for academic success. When you get out on your own, you'll have more decisions to make and more responsibilities to bear. Problems may be more complex and solutions more complicated.

However, don't let yourself believe that bigger problems and more responsibilities only produce greater frustrations. On the contrary, they can be energizers—creative ways to put your critical thinking skills to work for you.

Think of each problem or responsibility as a challenge. Then think of solving that problem or assuming that responsibility as a goal you can accomplish. As you apply the principles of goal setting, task management, priority setting, and problem solving to life's challenges, you will manage your life well and live with real confidence.

Thinking for the Future

Critical thinking is one of your most powerful strategies in a world that is constantly changing. Even in the 21st-century workplace, where job requirements are constantly shifting, you can still depend on your ability to think critically. In addition to basic skills and some personal qualities, employers are looking for people who can think.

In addition, when it's time for you to commit to a career and an employer, critical thinking will make your decision a choice, not just something that happens by default. More importantly, your decisions will be based on well-defined values that have passed through your filter of good reasoning.

In 1971, Golda Meir, the fourth prime minister of Israel, visited the elementary school she attended as a child in Milwaukee, Wisconsin. When she spoke to the school children there, she didn't speak about book learning. Even though she had excelled in academics, she admitted that she had learned a lot more in school than fractions or spelling.

In Meir's speech, she told the children how important it is to decide on the *way* they want to live. She encouraged them to get involved in causes that will help others. Then she told them essentially that what they would become would happen naturally—their career would develop smoothly when they put their values to work.

As you come full circle with the elements of critical thinking, you, too, may find that a career develops naturally. You will also see how your career and your other life decisions can have a positive effect. Whether you're defusing an argument among fellow students or finding a cure for diabetes, you will be making your mark on the world. Along the way, you will reap the personal benefits of sound, critical thinking.

> The most important motive for work in school and in life is pleasure in work, pleasure in its result, and the knowledge of the value of the result to the community.
>
> -Albert Einstein

Chapter 14
A MODEL FOR DECISION MAKING

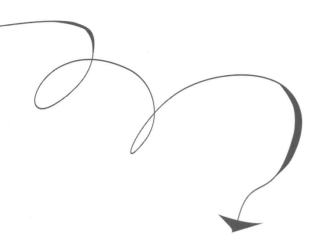

Life is full of decisions—little ones, big ones, easy ones, complicated ones. As you venture out into independent living for the first time, decision making will probably become more complex. Deciding what to have for breakfast and what to wear to school will be the small decisions you make every day. Other decisions may be much more difficult.

Making Decisions

Making a decision is a lot like solving a problem. In problem solving, you start with something you need to fix. In decision making, you start with a choice you need to make. In both cases, a person is at a starting place and needs to do something or change something in order to achieve an identified goal. The problem or decision is the space between where you are and where you want to be.

It's important to remember that pondering over a choice so long that you never make a decision is actually making a decision—you've decided not to do anything. This kind of "decision making" will never advance you very far.

> To decide, to be at the level of choice, is to take responsibility for your life and to be in control of your life.
>
> -Abbie M. Dale

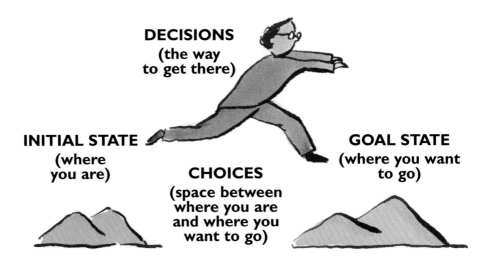

DECISIONS
(the way
to get there)

INITIAL STATE
(where
you are)

CHOICES
(space between
where you are
and where you
want to go)

GOAL STATE
(where you want
to go)

Many people have probably already asked you, *What are you going to do after graduation?* or *What kind of work do you want to go into?* By now, you've heard a lot of advice, but you know that the final decision is yours to make. Even though you may be anxious to make all of your own choices, some of the bigger decisions—like choosing a college, a major, and a career—may still feel a bit intimidating.

Some people have a sense of security when someone else makes big decisions for them. Then if things go wrong, they don't feel responsible and they have someone else to blame. Experienced critical thinkers, however, prefer to examine the evidence, reach their own conclusions, and confidently make their own choices. They know that there will be consequences, positive or negative, and they are equipped to deal with whatever comes their way.

Information—Your Point of Departure

With every choice that you face, there's a lot of information that you must deal with. It's your job to organize and analyze all relevant data before you make a firm decision. Some information that accompanies a choice is very obvious and clear. There is usually more information, though, that you will have to dig for. The following geometry example plainly illustrates this idea.

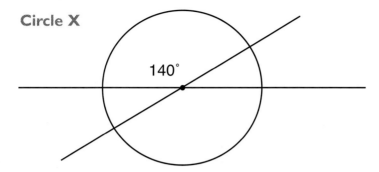

Circle X

140°

In this diagram, there are four angles—one is 140 degrees. That is the information that you are given. Even though the other three angles are not given, you can figure them out by using the basic laws of geometry. Thus, although the diagram appears to give you just the dimensions of one angle, it is actually giving you all four.

When you have to make a decision, first consider the obvious information. Then search for information that's not quite so apparent. There are several sources of information to consider when it comes to decision making: (1) information that comes with the decision; (2) information from your past knowledge and experience; and (3) information from relevant outside sources.

When you use all these sources of information to form patterns and hypotheses, you will come up with a new set of cumulative information—the information needed to make a decision with confidence.

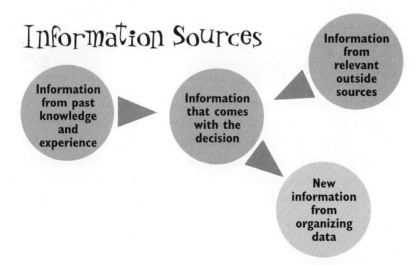

Information Sources

Information from past knowledge and experience

Information that comes with the decision

Information from relevant outside sources

New information from organizing data

In the following example, you'll get a chance to organize information and dig up new information by working with the given facts. First, see if you can solve the riddle on your own.

The Apartment Building
(An Exercise in Information Gathering)

Jed, Ted, Fred, Ned, Ed, Zed, Laura, Dora, Nora, Maura, Cora, and Flora are all tenants in the same six-floor apartment building. There are two apartments per floor. No more than two people live in any apartment. Some apartments may be empty.

For all six floors, list the tenants who live there and which people live together.

1. Ted and his roommate live two floors above Zed and his roommate Dora.

2. Jed lives alone, three floors below Ed and two floors below Cora.

3. Laura lives one floor below Zed and Dora.

4. Ned lives alone, three floors above the floor on which Nora and Maura have single apartments.

5. Flora and Fred live in single apartments, two floors below Laura.

Stumped?

Try this: For each of the five statements, make as many other statements as you can about the information that is not stated but implied. For example, for statement no. 1, the following additional information is implied:

   a. Neither Zed nor Dora are Ted's, nor anybody else's, roommate.

   b. Ted doesn't live on either the first or second floors. (If he did, how could he live two floors above Zed and Dora?)

Once you've done this for all the statements, look at your expanded set of information and see if you can solve the problem now.

ORGANIZE YOUR INFORMATION When information is given to you, it's usually not organized for the purpose of solving a problem. It's just there. If you want to use the information, you'll need to put some kind of order to it. It might be helpful to put it into categories, charts, or graphic representations. Look at the example again, this time with graphic representations. Notice how the graphics solve the riddle, step by step and clue by clue.

The Apartment Building
(Problem Solving with Graphic Representations)

Jed, Ted, Fred, Ned, Ed, Zed, Laura, Dora, Nora, Maura, Cora, and Flora are all tenants in the same six-floor apartment building. There are two apartments per floor. No more than two people live in any apartment. Some apartments may be empty.

For all six floors, list the tenants who live there and which people live together.

1. Ted and his roommate live two floors above Zed and his roommate Dora.

2. Jed lives alone, three floors below Ed and two floors below Cora.

3. Laura lives one floor below Zed and Dora.

4. Ned lives alone, three floors above the floor on which Nora and Maura have single apartments.

5. Flora and Fred live in single apartments, two floors below Laura.

Step 1 (use clue #1)

Ted and ?	?
?	?
Zed and Dora	?

Step 2 (use clue #3, then #5)

Ted and ?	?
?	?
Zed and Dora	?
Laura	?
?	?
Flora	Fred

Step 3 (use clue #4, then #2)

Ted and ?	Ed
Ned	Cora
Zed and Dora	[vacant]
Laura	Jed
Nora	Maura
Flora	Fred

With a riddle, information may indeed be the solution. However, with a real problem or decision, information is just your starting point—your point of departure. The next step is to clearly define the problem.

An undefined problem has an infinite number of solutions.

-Robert A. Humphrey

Houston, We Have a Problem

Problems cannot be solved at the same level of awareness that created them.

-Albert Einstein

In 1970, the crew of the Apollo 13 moon mission knew they had a problem when they heard a loud bang in the module. Yet until they gathered all the information available in order to clearly define the problem, they couldn't attempt to find a solution. When they determined that the service module oxygen tank was ruptured, they could then start to solve their problem and decide the best way to get back to Earth.

Take a look at the four basic steps in the following model for decision making. Notice that the first two steps match what the *Apollo 13* crew did to begin their decision-making process. Also notice that the process includes many of the basic elements of thought covered in Chapter 11.

Model for Decision Making

Identify the Problem or Choice

Decide what you need to solve or choose.
Define your goal.

Gather Relevant Information

Organize and analyze all relevant data.
Decide where to start.

Try out Solution Paths

Determine what options are available and hypothesize about their outcomes.
Look at the positives and negatives of each option.

Deal With Contingencies

If some paths contain problems, find a way around them.
If you can think of a more creative alternative, explore it.

Choose the Best Option

Choose and follow the best solution path to your goal.

Gathering information and identifying the problem or choice are often the easiest steps in the model for decision making. It is more difficult to come up with possible solution paths.

Solution Paths

More than likely, you'll arrive at a good decision every time if you take time to ask several *What if...?* questions. These questions explore hypothetical situations and suggest possible solution paths. When you come up with several solutions that you think might work, then imagine what life would be like if you were to choose each option. Look at the options one at a time.

For example, if you're trying to decide whether or not to accept a job offer, ask yourself questions like these: *What are the advantages of my taking this job? the disadvantages?* or *How will my taking this job benefit others? benefit me?*

Another good strategy is to write down all your possible choices and then discuss them with someone else—a friend, a relative, a counselor, a teacher, or a mentor. Compare their solutions with yours and ask them how they came to their conclusions. It's also a good idea to chart your choices on a pro/con T-chart or some other kind of graphic organizer.

As you sort through your options, be aware of what emotions are at work. Make an effort to focus only on those emotions that are relevant to your problem or choice. For example, the *Apollo 13* crew had to put aside their fear of being lost forever in space if they were going to have enough confidence and optimism to make the right decisions.

Choosing the Best Option

If you've carefully followed the first three steps of the Model for Decision Making, then choosing the best option will be fairly easy. Here's where you should be at this point:

- ~ You've clearly identified the problem or the choice you need to make.
- ~ You've organized and analyzed all the relevant information.
- ~ You've consulted with as many experts and resources as possible.
- ~ You've established some solution paths and put all options on the table.
- ~ You've hypothesized about the outcomes of your solution paths.
- ~ You've worked to use only relevant emotions to inform your decision.

If knowledge can create problems, it is not through ignorance that we can solve them.

-Isaac Asimov

I don't have any solution, but I certainly admire the problem.

-Ashleigh Brilliant

The best way to escape from a problem is to solve it.

-Alan Saporta

Now you're ready to choose the best option and make your decision. If you've predicted the various outcomes by asking *What if...?* questions and hypothesizing about possible solutions, you can have confidence in your decision. You will probably take some risks when you make a firm decision, but you will be able to move forward with determination since your decision is based upon concrete information and thoughtful reasons.

After you make a decision, it's a good idea to ask yourself, *Can I think of a better alternative?* If you still feel confident with your first choice, then you're probably on the right path.

APPLYING THE MODEL Now it's time for you to use the Model for Decision Making for one of your own problems or decisions. Don't forget to put into practice all the critical thinking skills you've already learned in this course. Here are just some of the things you can apply from the previous chapters.

- **Remember to look at the big picture.** For major decisions, you may need to envision yourself 10 or 20 years into the future.

- **Remember point of view.** How does this decision look from your point of view? Will anyone else's point of view be important in this decision?

- **Explore hypothetical situations.** *What if* I go to another college? *What if* I change my major? *What if* I accept this job offer?

- **Break down large decisions into a series of smaller decisions.** You can't make decisions for your entire life right now, but you can make decisions for next week, next month, next year.

- **Be persistent.** After you make a decision, do what it takes to carry it out. If you need to change your decision, be persistent in finding a better solution.

On a piece of paper, jot down several real problems or decisions you are facing right now or will be facing in the future. Now, choose one problem or decision from your list and use the following blank decision-making model to work your way to a final decision. Be sure to follow each step of the decision-making process, completing all four boxes.

Model for Decision Making

Identify the Problem or Choice

*Clearly state your problem or decision. Make sure
it is based upon information and data.*

Problem or Choice: _____

Information On Which It Is Based: _____

_____

Gather Information

List here all the relevant information you have about your issue or decision.

What is my issue or dilemma? _____

Relevant information:

_____   _____

_____   _____

_____   _____

Establish Solution Paths

List all your options and hypothesize about their outcomes.

Options	Hypothetical Outcome
1. _____	1. _____
2. _____	2. _____
3. _____	3. _____
4. _____	4. _____

Deal With Contingencies

Anticipate and plan solutions for problems. Imagine more creative alternatives.

Problems	Solutions
_____	_____
_____	_____

Better Ideas

_____

_____

_____

Choose the Best Option

Pinpoint and follow solution path to accomplish your goal.

My Best Option: _____

At first, decision making may seem like a long procedure, but after you use this model several times, the process will seem more natural. Eventually, you'll be thinking this way every time you're faced with a decision or a problem.

Avoiding the Obstacles

Obstacles cannot crush me. Every obstacle yields to stern resolve. He who is fixed to a star does not change his mind.

-Leonardo da Vinci

As you can see, making good decisions is a process anyone can master. Why, then, is the world filled with people taking wrong turns? It's because there are lots of "potholes" in their solution paths. In other words, while you're attempting to make a good decision, many obstacles can get in your way.

Being aware of obstacles is a crucial part of the decision-making process. Sometimes just being aware that the obstacles are there will help you navigate around them. Here are some of the more common things to watch out for.

Obstacle to Good Decision Making #1: Wishful Thinking

Most people are naturally optimistic. It's an important part of good decision making. However, when you build evidence on the side of an option you secretly prefer—instead of weighing the evidence objectively—that's just wishful thinking.

Example:

Mike has a serious cough that won't go away although he's been taking commercial cough medicine. He calls Dr. Jones who says, "Mike, I need to see you in my office as soon as possible to find out what's wrong."

Mike's best friend tells him, "Mike, you probably just have a cold. You know what doctors always say—get some rest and drink plenty of liquids."

What Mike's friend told him is probably what Mike wants to hear, but is it just wishful thinking? What decisions face Mike now?

_____

_____

Obstacle to Good Decision Making #2: Automatic Resistance

Critical thinkers like to make their own choices. Sometimes, when someone else makes a decision for you, emotion gets in the way of evaluating the decision. When your freedom to decide is taken from you, it's normal to resist, even if the decision imposed on you is a good one.

Example:

Carmella has narrowed down her two college choices to a college in her hometown and a large state university out of town.

One day her mother says, "Your dad and I have decided you must enroll in the college here in town. We're afraid you won't study as well in a residence hall. Besides that, college will be much more affordable if you can live at home."

All of a sudden, Carmella loses her freedom to decide. She's furious, although she secretly agrees with their reasoning, at least for her freshman year.

How might Carmella use her critical thinking skills to evaluate the decision that is imposed on her? How might she plan a reasonable dialogue with her parents that will examine all options and their possible outcomes?

_____

_____

_____

_____

_____

_____

Obstacle to Good Decision Making #3: Unclear Goals

Sometimes decisions are difficult to make because your goals might be unclear. A good decision must be goal-oriented. If you don't have any specific goals for your future yet, try focusing on a general, positive direction.

Example:

Ahmad does not know what he wants to major in once he enrolls in college. He does know how important it is to continue his education, so he makes plans to do so.

In college, he finds out that many other students are in the same boat.

Ahmad enrolls in General Studies until he can decide on a major. In the meantime, he makes it his plan to finish college.

What goals do you have that are still unclear? What general direction can you focus on until your goals become clear?

_____

_____

Obstacle to Good Decision Making #4: Fear of Failure

> The greatest mistake you can make in life is to be continually fearing that you will make one.
>
> -Ellen Hubbard

Some people think, "If I don't decide, then I can't make a mistake." If you think about it, procrastination and no action at all are types of decisions. They are decisions to put something off or not do anything at all.

Example:

Think of an instance when you experienced negative consequences because you procrastinated.

Think of an instance when <u>not</u> making a decision turned out to your benefit.

_____

_____

In what area have you decided not to make any decision at all? What do you think is keeping you from making a decision? How could you apply the model for decision making to this decision?

_____

_____

What specific decision have you been putting off? Experiment with a model for decision making for that decision.

_____

Obstacle to Good Decision Making #5: Task Management Problems

Sometimes people don't make good decisions merely because they don't take the time to work through the information and determine their options. You may need to make an effort to fit decision making into your task management plan.

Another obstacle to decision making is trying to plan your whole life right now. Determine which decisions have to be made right away and which ones can wait until next month or even next year.

Make a list of all the decisions you need to make or are even thinking about. Then prioritize them with a 1, 2, or 3 (1=needs to be made right now; 2=can wait a while; 3=can be made next year or later.)

_____

_____

_____

_____

_____

Summary

- -

Good critical thinkers make confident decisions because they base their choices on relevant information. The model for decision making in this chapter is one way you can make sure your decisions are based on good critical thinking.

Decision making is much like problem solving—for both, you must get from your initial state (where you are) to your goal state (where you want to go). Decisions are the way to get there. Whether you're deciding on what pair of shoes to buy or what college to attend, good decision making is based on fact, not done by chance.

One of your most powerful decision-making tools is organizing and analyzing information. Once you've gathered data from past knowledge and experience and other relevant sources, you can combine it with the information that comes with a decision to form new, helpful data. After defining the problem, pertinent information is the first important step in solving it.

> Not everything that is faced can be changed, but nothing can be changed until it is faced.
>
> —James Baldwin

Equipped with relevant data, now you can clearly define your problem or the choice you have to make. Solution paths—or options—become clear as you hypothesize about each possible choice. Trying to focus only on relevant emotions to affect your decision-making process will keep you from making impulsive choices.

You'll also want to be prepared to avoid any obstacles that may divert your attention away from good decisions. Some of the most common obstacles are wishful thinking, automatic resistance, unclear goals, fear of failure, and task-management problems. If you can avoid the traps that hinder good choices, you'll be well on your way to a rock-solid decision.

The hardest part of decision making is, of course, choosing the best option from all possible solution paths. However, with all the facts exposed and the problem and options clearly defined, the right decision is usually apparent. Sometimes you'll come up with a better alternative later, but a decision based on critical thinking is the winning choice. Once you've made your choice, you can confidently go on your way, carrying out your decision and reaching your goals.

Let's Talk

1. How does charting or diagramming a decision as you did on the Model for Decision Making help you choose the right solution path?

2. Explain how the elements of thought (see Chapter 11) are essential to good decision making.

3. What role does persistence play in making decisions?

Apply the Concepts

1. Apply the decision-making process to the following conflict-resolution situation. *People at school are gossiping about your best friend. They have the story wrong. You know the truth, but your friend shared it in confidence with you. Still, you feel strongly that you should set the record straight.* Using the Model for Decision Making, work through the decision-making process, showing all your steps. What is the best decision you could make in this situation?

2. Put yourself in this situation: *You receive an "incomplete" in your drawing class because your instructor says you didn't take the final exam. You did take the final exam and you have the drawing at home, but there's no grade on it.* Use the Model for Decision-Making to come up with a good plan for solving this dilemma. Show each step in your decision-making process.

3. Using the Model for Decision Making, analyze the following problem: *Too many people under the age of 21 drink alcohol. How can we reduce the number of underage drinkers?* Be sure to include all possible solution paths. Choose the best option. Explain your choice.

4. Put yourself into the following situation: *You are living in a dorm during your first year of college. Lately, you have been very homesick and you're finding it difficult to concentrate on your studies. You regret that you decided to go away to college and wish you could go back in time and make a different decision—to go to your hometown community college and live at home.* Using the Model for Decision Making, work through the entire process to come up with the best decision.

Choosing a career is one of the biggest decisions you will make. Identifying your best career choice can be a confusing task. Yet it can also be a very interesting and rewarding process if you apply the principles of critical thinking to your decision.

There is always room at the top.

-Daniel Webster

Finding Your Future

You may be the kind of person who knows, without question, what your college major will be and what career you want to pursue. Very few people, however, have such a strong **vocation**. Many people find it difficult to decide what kind of career they want.

vocation
a strong impulse to follow a particular career

If you don't have a strong vocation, you'll also find it problematic to declare a college major. Students sometimes change their majors more than once before feeling comfortable with their final choice. Even with careful planning, you may have to change your plans at some point.

For example, if you enjoy psychology courses in high school, you might choose that as your major in college. In the middle of the first term, however, you might discover that your college psychology courses with their emphasis on biochemistry are presenting a tremendous challenge that you aren't prepared to meet. This dilemma could make you reconsider your choices.

Sometimes outside circumstances require you to change directions. For instance, advancing technology might make your job choice in a particular field obsolete, thus forcing you to switch your focus. Competition in a particular profession might increase so much while you're in college that your chances for a job after you graduate become very uncertain.

You also might want to change your plans just because you develop different interests. A fascinating new career that didn't exist when you first declared your major might catch your attention halfway through college. Using the principles of critical thinking will make mid-course changes much easier in all these circumstances. Either you will have satisfactory reasons to make the change, or you will see the wisdom of your original plan.

Exploring Your Career

Take a few minutes to scan through the previous chapters of this course. As you recall what you've already learned and applied, ask yourself how the information relates to choosing and planning a career.

Here are some sample questions you might ask yourself.

~ *What activities put my natural learning drive into action?*

~ *In what subject is it easiest and most enjoyable for me to understand concepts and explore options?*

~ *In what subject am I motivated to learn more than what is required?*

~ *What is my learning style? Am I more right-brained or left-brained? Is the vocation I am exploring naturally compatible with my learning style? If not, can I make the necessary adjustments?*

~ *What is my dominant intelligence, and what kind of jobs match it?*

~ *In what course(s) do I excel academically?*

~ *Have I charted some possible career decisions using the Model for Decision Making?*

There is no future in any job. The future lies in the man who holds the job.

-George Crane

A good way to start planning your career is to pinpoint your main interests. The simple flowchart below shows how a job choice starts with your interests, points you to a particular field, then to a related profession, and finally to a specific job.

This sample reflects someone who enjoys and excels academically in high school English, edits the student newspaper, and likes to play sports. Notice how that information flows naturally to several professions.

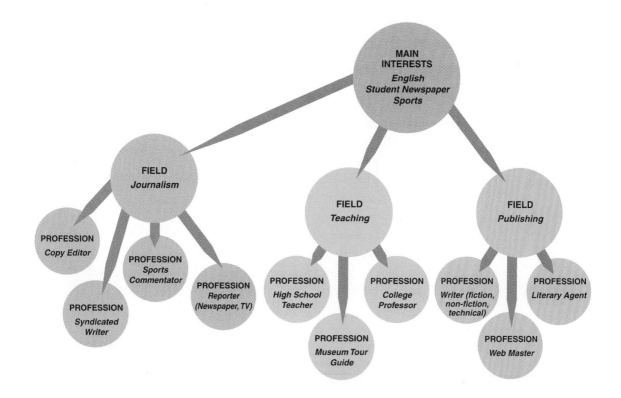

Now make your own flowchart. You'll need to start by identifying your main interests and determining careers that match them. You may then need to ask some questions or do some exploring to discover what fields, professions, and jobs match your interests.

Work is the rent we pay for the space we occupy on earth.

-Queen Elizabeth

Identifying Your Major

DEGREE POSSiBiLiTiES College-bound students typically ask, *What degree is required for my chosen career?* This is an important question because not all careers require a four-year degree. Some professions require much more than a four-year degree. Here is a summary of the possibilities.

Degree and Certificate Possibilities

Certificate — usually a one-year program in office, health services, technical, or mechanical fields (sometimes a license is required for certain jobs)

Associate's Degree — a two-year degree from a community or junior college

Bachelor's Degree — a four-year degree from a college or university

Graduate Degree (Master's or Doctorate) — requires additional years of school (post-graduate work following a four-year degree) that include comprehensive examinations, practical work, research, and written theses.

Professional Degree — requires additional years of school (a four-year degree plus post-graduate work) to qualify for professional fields such as engineering, law, medicine, higher education, advanced library information science.

The degree you choose to earn should depend on the level you want to achieve in a given field. For instance, if you enjoy secretarial work and plan to make it your career, you may only need a one-year certificate from a business school. Other business professions, such as accounting or computer programming, will probably require a bachelor's degree. If your goal is a management position in a larger company, it will help to have a master's degree.

CHOOSING A MAJOR Choosing a major represents a huge commitment and it is not uncommon for students to struggle with this decision. You will find that colleges offer courses and majors in fields you may never have heard of, so your last two years of high school can be a good time to explore academic majors and their opportunities and restrictions.

In the last few years, more high school counselors have urged students to consider taking general degrees in the core liberal arts. The reason? Technology is evolving so rapidly that a specific degree in a technological field may become obsolete, whereas a liberal arts degree can provide the general problem-solving background needed for all fields, including

Every day I get up and look through the *Forbes* list of the richest people in America. If I'm not there, I go to work.

-Robert Orben

technological ones. The main thing to keep in mind is that your degree provides just a launching pad for the continuous training and learning you'll do throughout all your working life.

Your last few years of high school are also a good time to research the vast number of jobs available to you and the prerequisite requirements for each one. So far, you've pinpointed your interests, connected them to a profession, and matched the profession to a degree level and a major.

CONNECTING A SPECIFIC JOB TO YOUR MAJOR Now imagine yourself at the beginning of your senior year in college. You're well on your way to receiving your degree in your chosen major. You have a good idea of the field you want to pursue. It's time now to discover what jobs are actually available in your chosen profession with the degree you'll soon earn. You might check the classified ads of your newspaper, job placement services, or Internet job-search sites. The following sites offer gateways to many job-related pages on the World Wide Web.

America's Career InfoNet (www.acinet.org)

Career Path (www.careerpath.com)

Headhunter.net (www.headhunter.net/index.htm)

JobBank USA (www.jobbankusa.com)

JobSearch.com (www.jobsearch.com)

Monster.com (www.monster.com)

The Occupational Outlook Handbook (www.jobweb.org/occhandb.htm)

The Riley Guide (www.dbm.com/jobguide/)

You can also check in the library for books like *The Encyclopedia of Associations*, which lists all the national professional organizations by field and key words. If you have a specific company in mind that you would like to work for, try searching their Web site for a list of employment opportunities.

Take some time to fill out your own chart like the one below. It is a simple, yet productive, tool for discovering specific career options and their hiring requirements. The digging and exploring will be well worth your time.

Exploring Academic Majors and Careers

Academic Major	Job Opportunities It Leads To
_____	_____
_____	_____
_____	_____
_____	_____

Available Job	Hiring Requirements
_____	_____
_____	_____
_____	_____

> Life consists not in holding good cards but in playing those you hold well.
>
> -Josh Billings

TALKING TO EMPLOYERS In your senior year of college, or even sooner, you'll probably start talking to potential employers. Many companies send job recruiters right to campus to interview student candidates. Employers sometimes hire students as summer interns and then consider them for full-time employment after graduation.

It's a good idea to talk to several employers before you graduate or accept a job. Because interviewing is a time-consuming process, you'll want to get an early start and not wait until your last month or so of school.

> Work to become, not to acquire.
>
> -Elbert Hubbard

When you do get a job offer, remember to use your critical thinking skills to decide if it is really the right job for you. Even though you might be flattered by an offer for a position, be sure the job matches your interests, draws on your skills, and supports your personal values and long-term life goals.

KEEPING UP WITH PROGRESS Because you're going to be in the midst of a fast-changing workforce, things may be very different in your chosen field by the time you graduate from college. It's important to keep up with the progress being made in your field. From time to time, you need to envision where you might fit into the picture when you receive your degree. Keep asking yourself, *Are my career plans and my major still relevant to my chosen profession?*

As a 21ˢᵗ-century worker, you'll need flexibility and creativity to survive in a workplace that is constantly changing and advancing. What worked in the 1900s will not work in the 2000s, and the workforce in 5, 10, or 20 years will undoubtedly be very different from what it is now. Notice how workers of the past (Industrial Age workers) compare to workers of today (Information Age workers).

In the late 1980s, some students in nursing programs at the State University of New York discovered that they could raise their eventual salaries by more than $25,000 per year if they took specialized training to assist at open-heart surgeries. When they entered the nursing program, this option wasn't even available. These students learned the importance of continuing to stay abreast of new options in their chosen field.

Industrial Age Workers	Information Age Workers
Depend on supervisor	Assume personal responsibility; shared leadership
Listen	Communicate
Follow orders	Make decisions; solve problems
Compete (personal power)	Cooperate (shared goals)
Product-oriented (factory)	Process- or people-oriented (global)
Follow routines (security)	Innovative (risk-taking)
Boss-oriented	Team-oriented
Highly defined job	Project-based assignments
Information filters down from management	Information received directly, frequently, online
Rule-bound; slow	Flexible; responsive
"Tell me what to do"	"Here's what I can do"
Resistant to change	Constantly learning

Amidst all the changes, however, remember again that critical thinking skills don't change. They adapt well to a changing work environment and help you to meet the challenges of a fast-moving, competitive career. Notice how relevant critical thinking is when you're actually on the job.

Change before you have to.

-Jack Welch

Critical Thinking Skills on the Job

- ~ Your learning drive and motivation have a positive effect on your productivity.

- ~ Your ability to see things from different points of view strengthens your "people skills."

- ~ Your ability to gather information, formulate relevant patterns, and hypothesize conclusions makes you a valuable employee. You can see the "big picture" of the company's goals and you're able to project outcomes of the company's actions and initiatives.

- ~ Your ability to break down large goals into small, achievable tasks makes you a valuable organizational asset. You have the capacity to move your company's projects forward smoothly and reliably.

- ~ Your problem-solving and decision-making expertise establishes your leadership potential and enhances your progress.

- ~ Recognizing your learning style helped you choose a company and a position that matches your learning style and intelligence. You're a good "fit" with the company and your job.

Getting the Job You Want

Life begets life. Energy creates energy. It is by spending oneself that one becomes rich.

-Sarah Bernhardt

Whenever you are asked if you can do a job, tell 'em, "Certainly, I can!" Then get busy and find out how to do it.

-Theodore Roosevelt

Getting the job you want will take plenty of investigation and research on your part. You'll want to find out exactly what abilities you need to be competitive in the 21st-century workplace.

THE INTERVIEW Even though you know how well qualified you are for a job, you will need some way to prove that to a potential employer in an interview. You will have to make sure the interviewer finds out the full background of your education, your work experience, your personal qualities, and your skills. You'll also have to convince the interviewer that you're the best candidate for the position.

At the same time, you'll want to have a supply of good questions to ask so that you can determine if this is, in fact, the right company and the right job for you. As some people say, you should use an interview to hire yourself an employer. It's a good idea to be well prepared when the interviewer gives you a chance to ask questions.

Most often, you'll want to bring with you a transcript of your grades, a resume, letters of recommendation, and perhaps samples of your work. How you present yourself, how you answer the interviewer's questions, and how your documents look will be determining factors in the employer's decision to hire you.

THE RESUME A resume is a document that you design yourself to give an employer an overall record of your background and accomplishments. Often a resume is sent to an employer in advance of the interview. Other times, you'll bring it with you. Typically, a resume includes the following:

- Personal Information—name, address, telephone number, e-mail address.
- Career Objective
- Education
- Employment History
- Relevant Personal Accomplishments
- Personal or Work References (with names, addresses, and telephone numbers) (References are usually requested when you become a finalist for a position.)

THE PORTFOLIO You may also want to show an employer your professional or student portfolio. A portfolio is a collection of evidence that documents your accomplishments, skills, and potential in specific areas. Usually, a portfolio is a nicely bound booklet with a professional-looking cover although for some fields, a video format is more effective.

Artists, writers, graphic designers, performers, photographers, and others use portfolios to showcase their work. However, you can design a portfolio for any field. Your portfolio should match your area of interest and highlight how you've prepared yourself for a particular kind of job or profession. Here are some ideas of what to include in your portfolio.

Portfolio Suggestions

~ Personal biography

~ Educational background and accomplishments

~ Copy of college transcripts

~ Letters of recommendation (personal, school, work)

~ List of references with contact information

~ Newspaper clippings of achievements, community service, volunteer work

~ Samples of your work—make this the major part of your portfolio. Display what you can do (artwork, graphic design, a computer program, audio or videotape of theatrical or musical performance, writing sample, photographs, etc.).

It's a good idea to start preparing a portfolio now and add to it as you progress through your education and work experience. Even if an employer does not ask specifically for a portfolio, you can still present one at the interview. Later on, if someone does request a sample of your background and your work, you will be prepared.

Keeping up with your portfolio also provides you with a "reality check" while you're in college. It is a good self-assessment tool for gauging your progress toward your goals.

Below is a Personal Portfolio Builder that will help you get started with your portfolio. It lists some general categories and ideas. Feel free to add other categories—it's up to you to tailor your portfolio to match your interests, abilities, skills, and the profession you are targeting. Below each category is a space for you to write down some specific ideas.

When you've completed your Personal Portfolio Builder, then get started putting together an actual portfolio that will represent who you are and where you're headed with your career.

Good hours, excellent pay, fun place to work, paid training, mean boss. Oh well, four out of five isn't bad.

-Help Wanted Ad

Personal Portfolio Builder

For each category, come up with some creative ideas for specific inclusions in your portfolio. These samples will provide evidence of your accomplishments in each category. You can tailor your portfolio for each interview by choosing the samples that fit the character of the job for which you are applying.

BASIC SKILLS—What evidence would demonstrate my accomplishments in these areas?

~ Reading   ~ Math   ~ Writing   ~ Speaking

Example: A major school project from a relevant academic area.

My portfolio pages _____

_____

THINKING SKILLS—What evidence would demonstrate my accomplishments in these areas?

~ Creative thinking   ~ Asking or answering questions   ~ Reasoning

~ Ranking, prioritizing   ~ Decision making   ~ Point of view

~ Problem solving   ~ Seeing the "big picture"

~ Hypothesizing   ~ Analyzing

Example: A chart listing alternative solutions that you identified for a particular problem and your reasoning for choosing one.

My portfolio pages _____

_____

PERSONAL QUALITIES—What evidence would demonstrate my accomplishments in these areas?

~ Responsibility   ~ Self-management   ~ Sociability

~ Integrity   ~ Honesty

Example: School attendance record, employer evaluations, letters of recommendation, character references.

My portfolio pages _____

_____

TECHNOLOGY SKILLS—What evidence would demonstrate my accomplishments in these areas?

~ Applying technology to task   ~ Software experience

~ Programming   ~ Maintaining and troubleshooting equipment

Example: Multimedia presentation placed on disk with description of technology used to integrate each component.

My portfolio pages _____

_____

Personal Portfolio Builder (continued)

INFORMATION—What evidence would demonstrate my accomplishments in these areas?

~ Acquiring, evaluating, organizing, maintaining, interpreting, and communicating information

~ Processing information using computers

Example: Survey results for a research project; video of an oral research presentation; list of Internet resources for a research project.

My portfolio pages _____

_____

INTERPERSONAL SKILLS—What evidence would demonstrate my accomplishments in these areas?

~ Team participation   ~ Teaching new skills to others

~ Serving clients, customers   ~ Exercising leadership

~ Negotiating   ~ Working with people with diverse backgrounds

Example: Statements from people you've worked with, led, or served (teammates, customers, students you've tutored, members of a group project)

My portfolio pages _____

SYSTEMS (interrelated things that form a complex or unified whole)—What evidence would demonstrate my accomplishments in these areas?

~ Understanding systems (organizational structures, long-range projects)

~ Monitoring and recording performance (charting progress, tracking success)

~ Improving and designing systems (changing structure to improve performance)

Example: An organization chart; a diagram illustrating how you analyzed and corrected a problem in a process, an organization, or a machine.

My portfolio pages _____

_____

    If you need help developing your portfolio, try contacting your college's career development office. Also look for software programs that are designed to help you create a resume and other portfolio pages. These are available on the World Wide Web and can be downloaded free or for a minimal charge.

When you assemble your portfolio, remember to be creative and to include a variety of elements. A booklet with page after page of text could be boring, whereas a picture or graphic highlight might help your materials to stand out from the rest.

ELECTRONIC INTERVIEWS Keep in mind that preliminary interviews can now be done electronically in many cases. A job opening posted on the Internet might enable you to paste your resume onto a company's automated application form. Or you might be invited to attach your resume to an e-mail communication. There are security concerns about serving resumes on the Internet, so if you choose to do this, make sure you don't mind that others know you are job hunting. If you give contact information, it's a good idea to transmit your resume via an encrypted (secure) system.

You may want to have your resume and your portfolio on computer. Pictures and samples of your work can be scanned and placed in your portfolio file. When you have a person-to-person interview, you may want to prepare a computer presentation on a software program like PowerPoint. Make sure your software is compatible with the company's computer system. It's a good idea to make a follow-up call to determine if your material downloaded correctly.

POINT OF VIEW Each time you submit a resume or portfolio to a potential employer, examine it from the hiring company's point of view. Include only the information that is relevant to the position and leave out anything in which the employer has no interest.

Find out if the company or organization is traditional, informal, or something in between. Then fashion your portfolio to match the character of the company. Imagine what the employer's first impression will be of you and of the materials you bring with you. First impressions count heavily in an application process, so you'll want to invest some care and time in your application process and materials.

CURRICULUM VITAE Curriculum vitae are a lot like a portfolio but are typically tailored to the academic, scientific, or publishing professions. Your educational credentials figure prominently in curriculum vitae, as do your research and writing experience and credentials.

If you're applying for a position in higher education, writing, or research, title your resume "Curriculum Vitae." Curriculum vitae are also enclosed with grant applications.

NETWORKING A productive job-hunting resource is your network. Your personal network consists of the people you know—and the people they know. Although we like to believe we can always get things accomplished on our own, we sometimes need the help of other people to find a job.

You may not think of yourself as having a network, but you do. Every person you know is in it, even your fellow students who might know someone who knows someone else who can direct you to a good position. In college, your network will expand significantly to include new friends and professors who will become valuable resources for career guidance and job connections. If you have a part-time job, work as an intern, or do volunteer work, the people you work with will also be good networking resources.

When Plans Go Awry

Thus far in *College Transition*, the stage has been set for success—a well-formulated college plan, ways to accomplish the plan, and a strategy for landing the ideal job in the career of your choice. It all sounds good—and it does work—but what happens when plans go awry?

One day, to your dismay, you may find that you are failing a college course. Or perhaps problems will arise in a personal relationship. Maybe a career plan you've had since childhood will lose its appeal when you actually tackle the required course work. You may end up worrying about disappointing your family if you make any changes.

At this point, it's time to summon all of your problem-solving and decision-making strategies. You may have to create an alternate plan that will better suit your abilities, your style, and your emotional and practical needs.

GETTING ACADEMIC HELP College years are widely acclaimed as the best years of your life, but at times you may not feel that way. Pressures inevitably mount during this time. Often it is assumed that you are an adult and will do what it takes to get help. First, you will need to know where to go for help.

Especially during your first year of college, you will need academic guidance. For example, if you've always wanted to be a doctor, but you're getting low grades in biology and chemistry, you may need to talk to a professor in the science department, an academic advisor, a family member, or a friend who's also majoring in pre-med.

When you go for help, be prepared to have a candid conversation about your situation and your options. Try to have some specific questions that will help you sort out the situation.

- Do I have the ability and the desire to persist?
- Where can I get additional help and counseling?
- How would it affect my life if I changed my major or career direction?
- Should I transfer to a different college or department?
- Should I change my major?

Remember, many college students change or adjust their goals at least once. If this happens to you, remember that change is not failure. It is part of the process of finding your right place in the world.

GETTING PERSONAL HELP Personal pressures may also sometimes feel overwhelming. Living in a residence hall may not be all you thought it would be, or social obligations might be very different from what you were used to in high school. You may suffer from homesickness. All the demands on your time may stress you out, or financial problems may weigh you down.

No matter what your problems are, they often seem bigger and more traumatic when you're also contending with heavy academic pressures. You may feel that there's no way out, but there are always options when you put your critical thinking strategies to work. When you view your personal problems through the filter of reason, you can make sound judgments and wise decisions.

If a personal problem approaches a crisis level, you should always seek help at once. Don't worry about appearing to overreact. Your only concern should be for your well-being and safety.

Most campuses have a student health service and a crisis intervention center. The college's office of public safety can also assist you if you perceive a threat or imminent danger. Your own quick decision-making skills will also help you in crisis situations.

The following list will give you some good ideas about where to go for assistance when you need it.

There is no quit in me.
-Larry Holmes

Walk away from it until you're stronger. All your problems will be there when you get back, but you'll be better able to cope.
-Lady Bird Johnson

Trouble is a part of your life, and if you don't share it, you don't give the person that loves you enough chance to love you enough.
-Dinah Shore

Student Resources for Personal Help

Family members	Crisis intervention center
Office of public safety	Religious leaders
Academic advisors	Recent graduates
College resource center	Mentors
Residential advisors	Student handbook
Student health services	

Summary

College is an exciting place in which your decisions will have a definite impact on the rest of your life. Making your choices wisely by using your critical thinking skills will ensure that you have the best possible opportunities to live up to your potential.

One of the most important decisions you will make is what career you will pursue. Your choice of a profession starts by pinpointing your main interests. From there, you can narrow your choices down to relevant fields and professions. With some investigation, you can find out what degree is required for the job you want and plan your course of study accordingly. When you know what profession you're interested in, you can declare an appropriate major.

You will need to keep up with the many changes that are taking place in your field of study so that you'll remain competitive after you graduate. Flexibility and creativity are important qualities for a 21st-century worker. In spite of all the workplace changes, though, the demand for good critical thinking skills never changes. Your ability to solve problems and work easily through a decision-making process will ensure that you remain a valuable employee.

When you're well on your way to completing the educational part of your plan, then you can advance to the next phase—getting the job you want.

Being well prepared for an interview is the first step. You'll need to prepare a high-quality resume, vitae, or portfolio to introduce yourself to the prospective employer. Every aspect of your application process will reflect who you are and why you will be a valuable asset to a company or organization.

Although plans keep you on track and keep you going in the right direction, sometimes things go awry. When that happens, it's not the time to declare failure—it's time to put your critical thinking strategies to work and create an alternate plan.

Personal dilemmas sometimes necessitate choices and changes. However, when you apply your problem-solving skills and use available resources, you will make wise decisions and ultimately achieve your goals.

Let's Talk

1. What do you think the best course of action is when you want to change your academic plans? Describe each step you would take.

2. What is your most likely vocation? What specific profession will most likely fit your vocation? What college major would best prepare you for that profession?

3. Discuss several ways you can keep up with the changes that are taking place in your chosen profession. Be specific.

4. Why do critical thinking skills survive in a fast-changing workplace? List specific reasons.

5. What do you think is the most important part of a job application process? Explain your answer.

Apply the Concepts

1. Visit the library or search the Internet to find out what predictions have been made for the 21st-century workplace. Determine which changes have already taken place in our society. Then, pretend you are living 15 years in the future and write an imaginary letter to a high school friend describing what kind of work you've been doing since graduation.

2. Obtain a course catalog from a college you're thinking about attending. Be sure you get a catalog that lists all the majors the college offers and the courses required for each major. Now identify three majors you are interested in and find out what courses are required for degrees in those majors. Then answer these questions:

    (a) *How closely do the courses resemble ones you've taken already in high school?*

    (b) *What requirements surprise you (if any)?*

    (c) *If you start work in one major and change your mind after a year, which of the three majors appears to have the most courses that would transfer to another major? Which major has the least?*

3. Picture yourself having just received your degree in one of the three majors you identified in question 2 above. Explain what types of jobs you are now qualified for. Choose one general career area and examine the specific jobs in it. Then conduct an interview with someone who works in that type of job. Find out what their work consists of and what experience and training they received to qualify for the job.

4. Based on your research in questions 2 and 3 above, answer the following questions:

    (a) *If you obtain your desired degree, what jobs will you be qualified for? Which ones would you be happy doing?*

    (b) *Are there many openings in these jobs?*

    (c) *Are there openings in your geographic area, or might you have to move?*

    (d) *Are these jobs that people typically stay in for a long period of time and that have opportunity for advancement—or do people usually leave after a few years?*

    (e) *Would you modify your present college plans based on what you have just found out?*

Epilogue
Making Your Mark in the World

You've finished the *College Transition* course. Congratulations! Now you're ready to go out and make your mark on the world.

Will critical thinking always help you, even when you're out in the mainstream of society and involved in a career? The answer is *yes*. Even though you operate from a complicated array of influences—mind, emotions, and circumstances—you can employ carefully ordered thinking to navigate successfully through a complex and rapidly changing world.

MAKING COMMON SENSE "COMMON" *College Transition* is basically about looking at the facts, weighing your options, imagining their outcomes, and using your reasoning abilities to come to rational conclusions. Some people call this "common sense," but, at times, *sense* isn't all that *common*. This is why we have to utilize our critical thinking skills and make common sense a common part of our lives.

When you put critical thinking to work for you, your academic life becomes easier and your thought processes rise to higher levels. Your career becomes a choice rather than just a chance, and living on your own becomes an exciting challenge instead of a stressful burden.

You're probably already reaping the benefits of critical thinking with elevated academic performance and better personal decision making. There are even more benefits to come. There may be times at college when you feel stressed out or teeter on the brink of quitting. With the strategies you've learned in this course, you'll be able to look hard at your circumstances, analyze them, and determine the possibilities that will get you back on track. Always remember to search for your options.

No one's life proceeds in a straight line. Even very successful people find that the path of life is full of curves, dips, and detours. The important thing to remember is that you have the necessary tools and strategies to decide for yourself—at every curve, dip, or detour—what your best option is.

MAKING A DIFFERENCE IN THE WORLD As you follow your path, you will undoubtedly meet others who are struggling. You may, at some point in your life, feel a responsibility to help out, perhaps right on your campus or maybe on the other side of the world. Your abilities and skills can definitely make a positive difference.

Here are just some of the volunteer opportunities available to you.

Habitat for Humanity

Special Olympics

Literacy Volunteers

Big Brothers and Sisters

The American Red Cross

St. Jude's Hospital

Amnesty International

Doctors Without Borders (the Nobel-Prize-winning group that treats needy patients all over the world)

Below are several Web sites that will connect you with some additional worthwhile social causes.

Where to Give — www.wheretogive.org

Doctors Without Borders — www.dwb.org

International Rescue Committee — www.intrescom.org

American Red Cross — www.redcross.org

HOPE Worldwide — www.hopeww.org

Oxfam America — www.oxfamamerica.org

Whatever mark you decide to make on the world, we encourage you to keep using the resources within you to think critically through every choice, make sound decisions, and accomplish your goals. Have a happy and very successful future.

> Life is a series of experiences, each one of which makes us bigger, even though it is hard to realize this. For the world was built to develop character, and we must learn that the setbacks and griefs which we endure help us in our marching onward.
>
> -Henry Ford

> We make a living by what we get, we make a life by what we give.
>
> -Sir Winston Churchill

> Life is no brief candle to me. It is a sort of splendid torch which I have got a hold of for the moment, and I want to make it burn as brightly as possible before handing it on to future generations.
>
> -George Bernard Shaw

Resources

You may be very good at identifying problems and even solving them. Your task would be much easier, though, if you were aware of all the useful resources available to help you get things done. The following information and list of resources will be helpful as you move on to the college of your choice and to life on your own.

Standardized Tests

Although you've probably heard a lot about college entrance tests, you may not know what each one is. Check with colleges you are interested in to see which college entrance tests you are required to take.

PSAT/NMSQT (Preliminary Scholastic Aptitude Test/National Merit Scholarship Qualifying Test)—This is a test that helps you prepare for the SAT. It is usually administered in 10th or 11th grade. Although colleges do not see your score, if you do well on this test, you may qualify for the National Merit Scholarship Program. Preparing for the PSAT is an excellent way to practice for the SAT.

SAT I (Scholastic Assessment Test)—This test measures your aptitude in mathematical and verbal comprehension and problem solving. Many colleges require students to submit their test scores when they apply for admission. You probably will want to take this test when you are a junior. If you are not satisfied with your score, you may then retake it when you are a senior.

ACT (American College Testing Assessment Test)—This test, like the SAT, measures a student's aptitude in mathematical and verbal comprehension and problem solving. Some colleges require students to take the ACT, while others require the SAT. Most students take the ACT during their junior or senior year or during both years.

SAT II (Scholastic Assessment Test)—These achievement tests, offered in many specific areas of study, are required by some colleges when you apply for admission in certain fields.

Financial Aid

On most college campuses, there is an Office of Financial Aid that assists students with state, federal, and private financial aid awards. There are basically two kinds of financial aid: need-based and merit-based.

NEED-BASED AID

1-800-4FED-AID —Call this number to request a financial aid student guide.

Free Application for Federal Student Aid and/or Financial Aid Form (FAFSA/FAF) —Your high school or the colleges you are interested in should have a supply of these forms. They are applications your parents or guardians must fill out if they are claiming special hardship circumstances.

Grants —There are numerous federal, state, and private sector grants available. They are usually awarded based on need. The money does not have to be paid back.

MERIT-BASED AID

Merit Scholarships —Check with your high school counselor to find out what private sector or campus-based scholarships are available in your area or in your state.

WORK/STUDY PROGRAMS

Many colleges offer work/study programs as part of a financial aid package. The jobs are usually based on campus, and the money earned is meant to be used to pay your tuition or other college expenses. Work/study aid can be need-based, merit-based, or a combination of both.

STUDENT LOAN PROGRAMS

Student loans typically have a very low interest rate and payments don't start until after you graduate. If you decide to apply for a student loan, keep in mind that you will have to pay it back—it is not a gift. Also think of it as an investment with very long-lasting benefits.

Special Needs

If you are a student served by the Americans With Disabilities Act, you will need to ensure that you receive all services available to you on your college campus. Most colleges have a student services office for disabled people. You will want to find out about your college's Individualized Education Program (IEP) that will tailor your program to meet your needs.

Course Materials —If course material is not in a format you can use, ask your college to provide you with a readable format (large print, Braille, tape, computer disk). This is your right as a citizen of the United States.

Adaptive Computers —Many specialized computers and programs offer features like large-print screens, voice activation, and speech software that will speak what's printed on the computer screen.

Testing Modifications —As part of the Individualized Education Program (IEP), your tests can be modified to give you extra time, a distraction-free environment, a scribe to write your answers, a person to read your test, and the use of a calculator.

Accessibility —Ask your college to ensure that all buildings and services you need are accessible to you.

Index

A

B

C

Perfectionism, 52

Persistence, natural learning drive and, 9

Personal help, 275–276

Personal Portfolio Builder, 270–272

Perspective, 23

Persuasion, 194. *See also* Argumentation

Persuasion mode, 214

Pessimism, 52

Plagiarism, 232

Planning
  of career, 262–263
  for critical thinking, 41–43
  to get job you want, 268–274
  help sources and, 274–276
  of major, 263–268
  for multitasking, 76–77
  for task achievement, 71–74
  of time during tests, 160

Point of view
  in critical thinking, 175, 176, 178, 179,
    180, 185–188
  of resumes and portfolios, 273

Portfolios, 269–273

Power, from critical thinking, iv

Preliminary Scholastic Assessment Test
  (PSAT), resources for, 281

Priorities, setting, 78–82

Process mode, 214, 215

Professional degrees, 264

Proofreading, 230–231

Properties of mind, 1–3. *See also* Action;
  Drive; Openness; Reason

Purpose, in critical thinking, 175, 176,
  178, 179, 180, 185–188

Q

Qualifiers, in objective test questions, 152

Question at issue, in critical thinking, 175,
  176, 178, 179, 181, 185–188

Questions
  asking before reading, 132–134
  for career planning, 262
  in disciplines, 123–124
  levels of, 120–123
  shaping, for writing, 219
  summary, preparing from notes,
    130–131
  on tests. *See* Test taking
  turning notes into, 127

R

Random thinking, 40

Rationales, 196–203
  categories of, 196–200
  fallacies and, 106–203
  in writing, 222

Reading
  key words and, 112
  processing before, 132–134

Realistic goals, 64, 66

Reason, 2, 3, 36–44. *See also* Critical
  thinking
  applying to life, 42
  applying to work, 43
  filtering choices and, 39–40

Reasoning
  analogic, 200
  causal, 199
  circular, 203

Red herrings, 202

References, keeping track of, 220

Repertoire, 49

Research, preliminary, for writing, 218

Resistance, automatic, as obstacle to
  decision making, 255

Resumes, 269

Retention, 106, 107–109

Retrieval, 106, 110–114

Textbook reading, key words and, 112

Theoretical situations, 157

Theses, 212

Thesis statements, 223

Thinking, 170
    critical. *See* Critical thinking
    graphic organizers for, 134–142
    hypothetical, 25–26, 28–29
    importance of, 189–190
    open. *See* Openness
    random, 40
    right brain/left brain, 92–97
    transferable, 189
    wishful, as obstacle to decision making, 254

Time
    task management and, 71–74
    test taking and, 160

Tone, in writing, 227

Transferable thinking, 189

True-false test questions, 152
    tips for, 158

U

Uncertainty, open thinking and, 25–26, 29

Unclear goals, as obstacle to decision making, 256

Urgency, priority setting and, 78, 79

V

Value, motivation by, 56–58

Verbal/linguistic intelligence, 99

Viewpoint
    in critical thinking, 175, 176, 178, 179, 180, 185–188
    of resumes and portfolios, 273

Visibility, priority setting and, 78, 80

Visualization, as memory hook, 114

Visual-spatial intelligence, 99

Vocation, 261. *See also* Career planning; Job *entries*

Voice, in writing, 226

Volunteer opportunities, 280

W

Web sites
    job-related, 265
    for locating volunteer opportunities, 280

Weight, priority setting and, 78, 80

Will, 48

Wishful thinking, as obstacle to decision making, 254

Work. *See also* Career planning; Job *entries*
    applying reason to, 43

Work/study programs, 282

Writing, 210–235
    critical, elements of, 212–224
    critical thinking and, 224
    documentation and attribution in, 232–234
    editing and, 225–231
    managing process of, 215–224
    power of, 211–212